WORLD
CHAMPION
COMBINATIONS

ABOUT THE AUTHORS

Grandmaster Raymond Keene, multiple tournament winner, and former British Champion, is the world's most prolific chess writer, with more than 100 books to his credit. Considered one of the strongest players in the world and one of the top theoreticians, Keene is well known for his work organizing world championships, his many best-selling chess titles, and for his co-authorship with World Champion Garry Kasparov and Eric Schiller on *Batsford Chess Openings* - the all-time best-selling reference work on chess openings.

Keene is a former British champion and medal winner in the chess Olympiad, and was awarded the title Officer of the British Empire, by Queen Elizabeth II for his services to chess. He is the chess correspondent for the Spectator, London (since 1977), and Thames Television (since 1986), and writes the London Times daily chess column. Keene's new book for Cardoza Publishing, *Cardoza's Complete Book of Beginning Chess*, is due out in Fall 1998.

Eric Schiller, widely considered one of the world's foremost chess analysts, writers and teachers, is internationally recognized for his definitive works on openings. He is the author of 80 chess books including Cardoza Publishing's definitive series on openings, *World Champion Openings*, *Standard Chess Openings*, and *Unorthodox Chess Openings*—an exhaustive opening library of more than 1700 pages. He's also the author of *Encyclopedia of Chess Wisdom, Gambit Opening Repertoire for White, Gambit Opening Repertoire for Black, Complete Defense to King Pawn Openings, Complete Defense to Queen Pawn Openings*, and multiple other chess titles for Cardoza Publishing. (For listings of all chess titles published by Cardoza Publishing, go online to www.cardozapub.com.)

Eric Schiller is a National and Life Master, an International Arbiter of F.I.D.E., and the official trainer for many of America's top young players. He has also presided over world championship matches dating back to 1983.

WORLD CHAMPION COMBINATIONS

RAY KEENE & ERIC SCHILLER

Finish 'em off

CARDOZA PUBLISHING

ACKNOWLEDGEMENTS

The authors wish to thank Bill Haines and Gabe Kahane for their help in preparing and checking materials used in this book.

First Edition

Library of Congress Catalogue Card No: 97-65488
ISBN: 0-940685-77-9

TABLE OF CONTENTS

1. INTRODUCTION

The combination is the pinnacle of chess art, a creative fantasy that involves bold sacrifices uncompromisingly played with an advantage gained as a result. Combinations bring chess players a heady adrenaline rush, and are the pride and joy of every fan of the Royal Game. This book shows you the art of combination in the hands of the very best players of all time, the World Champions.

Combinations are part of most great games of chess, but are also found in battles that are otherwise uninteresting. They are found in decisive victories, but also appear in drawn games and those that are lost through subsequent errors. It is hard to visit a tournament and not see examples of combinative play. One of the earliest goals of any aspiring chessplayer is to learn to spot and execute combinations.

There is a widespread notion that the faculty of devising combinations in chess cannot be acquired, but depends rather on an inborn power of calculation and imagination. Every experienced player knows, however, that this general opinion is wrong, and that most combinations, indeed, practically all of them, are cooked up by recalling known elements, such as the famous bishop sacrifice on f7, or h7, which will not give the advanced player much to think about. That the power of combination can be developed by study really seems very natural if you think about both of its components separately. You can learn to perform the necessary mental gymnastics of calculation. As for the imagination which furnishes the necessary ideas and surprises for the combination, psychologists claim that it cannot offer anything absolutely new, but, contenting itself with combining familiar elements, can be developed by increasing knowledge of such elements.

In order to bring the art of the combination into your own games, you will need to study the instructive examples found throughout chess literature. The World Champions, are those players who have climbed the highest peaks of chess, have used combinations regularly throughout their careers. In this book we will examine the best and most enlightening examples of their craft.

Each of the World Champions (we will include American Paul Morphy as well as the 13 "official" champions) has a unique style, and the combinations which they create come in many flavors. From Morphy to Kasparov, the great players have launched combinations against opponents ranging from children to sophisticated computers. Using the patterns they have studied, they create fresh and brilliant gems at the chessboard. If you too study the classics, you'll find yourself composing similar masterpieces in your own battles.

2. WHAT IS A COMBINATION?

It may come as a surprise that this common term, *combination*, has no agreed upon definition in chess. Every chess player has the vague notion that a combination is a sequence of moves involving a successful sacrifice, where the enemy is doomed to suffer some damage, either materially or positionally. If we define the term too tightly, then we may exclude many worthy examples of chess artistry. At the same time, if we allow any sacrifice to count as a combination we will be opening the doors so wide that the honor of being dubbed a "fine combination" will be diminished.

Rather than provide a technical definition, we will let the examples of combinations as played by the World Champions enlighten us. To be sure, all of the combinations involve sacrifices, all leave the opponent with limited options, and all wind up bringing some tangible advantage to their creator. But what sort of advantage is required to justify the award? As Dr. George Steiner wrote in *Fields of Force* in the New Yorker back in 1972: "Such key concepts as 'advantage' and 'sound sacrifice' are far too indeterminate, far too subjective and historically fluid to be rigorously defined and formalized."

We agree with Dr. Steiner, and note further that a sacrifice is "sound" only after exhaustive investigation, which often takes place over decades. Powerful computers can now be used to check the accuracy of combinations and can often find tougher defenses or outright refutations, but in our opinion this does not lessen the artistic, sporting or instructional value of the game.

Indeed, you will find in our collection some examples where later research found flaws in the gems, but you will, we are sure, find the combinations artistically satisfying and instructive in any event. As for the sporting value, well, a win is a win, after all!

3. PAUL MORPHY

Paul Morphy (USA), Unofficial World Champion (1857–1859)

Paul Morphy was the greatest player of his time and although he is not among the officially recognized World Champions, it is only because the title did not exist at the time. The New Orleans native lived from 1837 until 1884, and his brief chess career has outlived him by over a century.

Morphy's rise is perhaps the most meteoric in chess history. When he went to Europe in 1858, he was not considered a threat to the great players of his day, such as Howard Staunton and Adolph Anderssen. By the end of the year he had blown away Anderssen and frightened off Staunton. He clearly demonstrated his domination of the game, and then, as Bobby Fischer would do over a century later, he simply stopped playing.

Morphy is remembered especially for his brilliant wins, but in fact his games were not of the highest quality. Defensive technique was terrible in the mid-19th century, and there was a strong, if unwritten, obligation to accept any sacrifice thrown one's way.

One must keep in mind, however, that chess theory was still in its early stages. Morphy was ahead of his time in his understanding of positional factors and his strategies were more in keeping with the demands of the position than was usual at the time. Morphy understood that there were important general principles which had to be followed if success was to come naturally at the board.

He realized that control of the center was a factor of major importance in the game. Morphy's openings concentrated on the development of forces and the creation of open lines for attack. With those goals achieved, opportunities for combinations would present themselves.

So, while we admire the stunning achievements of his best known games, we must keep in mind that his success was due in large part to the fact that his appreciation of the game and tactical prowess were so much greater than that of his contemporaries. Morphy didn't need to dig deep into his tactical arsenal. Nevertheless, he managed to whip up combinational finishes that were very impressive to chess fans of his time, and remain entertaining even today.

Let's start with a couple of examples where his opponents functioned as punching bags.

(1) MORPHY - E. MORPHY
New Orleans, 1849

1.e4 e5; 2.Nf3 Nc6; 3.Bc4 Bc5; 4.c3 d6; 5.0–0 Nf6; 6.d4 exd4?! This is a classic example of a premature capture in the center. White will obtain an ideal pawn center, and Black has no compensation. **7.cxd4 Bb6; 8.h3.** A useful move, keeping Black from placing pressure on the White center with ...Bg4. **8...h6.** Black reasons that if White could take "time out" for h3, he can do the same for ...h6. 8...0–0 would have been safer. **9.Nc3 0–0; 10.Be3 Re8.** Black seeks counterplay on the open file, but this leaves f7 weak.

11.d5 Bxe3. Black fails to appreciate the power of the bishop at c4. **12.dxc6! Bb6.** The bishop must retreat, or Black will find himself a piece down! **13.e5.** The point of this move is to weaken the coverage of e5 by Black, who now controls the square. Once the pawn captures, the control is lessened, and the square is only supported by a rook. **13...dxe5; 14.Qb3 Re7.**

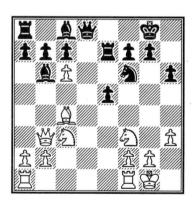

Morphy now uses a combination to exploit the powerful pin on f7. **15.Bxf7+! Rxf7.** Declining the sacrifice would also have lost. 15...Kh8; 16.Nh4 g5; 17.Ng6+ Kg7; 18.Nxe7 Qxe7; 19.Bd5 Nxd5;

20.Nxd5 Qf7; 21.Nxb6 axb6; 22.Qxf7+ Kxf7; 23.Rfc1 and Black is busted! 15...Kf8; 16.Rfd1! and White wins, for example: 16...dxc3; 17.cxb7 Rb8; 18.bxc8Q Qxc8; 19.Qc3. **16.Nxe5 Qe8; 17.cxb7.** The pin is eternal, and Black is lost. **17...Bxb7; 18.Rae1 Ba6.** This wins the rook at f1, but it hardly matters. **19.Ng6! Qd8; 20.Re7!** The final exploitation of the pin. **Black resigned.**

(2) PAULSEN - MORPHY
New York City, 1857

As a public relations effort Morphy's sixth game of his Finals Match with Louis Paulsen from New York, 1857, could hardly have been better. In his very first serious tournament Morphy not only gained top prize, but defeated his nearest rival, a European Master, by the score of five wins, two draws and only one loss, including the following brilliant queen sacrifice. A game played in such circumstances would have been quite sufficient to convince the chess fraternity of his day that Morphy's opponents were fated to perish from stunning combinations.

Lasker, however, viewing Morphy's achievements from a more distant and objective standpoint, attributed his success to the scientific application of logical principles, and his victories to a gradual development of forces which crushed his opponent with cumulative effect. The combinative element would arise naturally from his superior demonstration of chess generalship–it was not an untamed, demonic force, bursting wildly into flame every time Morphy's hand reached out to touch a piece.

1.e4 e5; 2.Nf3 Nc6; 3.Nc3 Nf6; 4.Bb5 Bc5. Fluid development typical of Morphy, but the symmetrical 4...Bb4 is more reliable.
5.0–0 0–0.

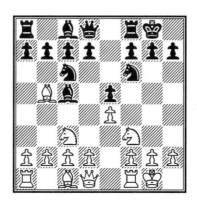

6.Nxe5. Introducing a simple exchanging combination, known as the "fork trick," e.g. 6...Nxe5; 7.d4. White stands better. **6...Re8; 7.Nxc6.** Not bad, since it impairs Black's queenside pawn structure, but the most incisive course is 7.Nf3 Nxe4; 8.d4 Nxc3; 9.bxc3 followed by d4-d5.

7...dxc6; 8.Bc4. Superior is 8.Be2, for Black now has the opportunity of introducing a powerful attack with 8...Ng4. **8...b5?!** Of course Morphy does not fall for our old friend 8...Nxe4?; 9.Nxe4 Rxe4; 10.Bxf7+ and 11. Qf3+. **9.Be2 Nxe4; 10.Nxe4 Rxe4; 11.Bf3.** Here Paulsen should have tried 11.c3 while his king bishop defended d3.

11...Re6.

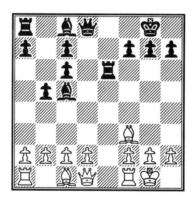

12.c3? The less ambitious 12.d3 is preferable. **12...Qd3!** To a modern player, it seems only natural to occupy this key square, simultaneously hamstringing White's development, but to Paulsen the move must have come as something of a revelation. Interestingly, White still has chances for successful resistance, even after this body-blow, a comment on the concealed resources of the chessboard.

13.b4 Bb6; 14.a4! bxa4; 15.Qxa4. The counter-idea emerges, but Paulsen implements it in a faulty fashion, since he underestimates the combinative potential of Black's position. **15...Bd7; 16.Ra2?** Pointless. With 16.Qa6 White can, at once, repair much of the damage.

16...Rae8; 17.Qa6. We doubt if Paulsen, or anyone else present at the Congress, had the slightest inkling of the shattering response Morphy had planned.

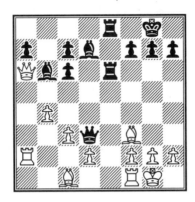

17...Qxf3!! The million dollar public relations move. **18.gxf3 Rg6+; 19.Kh1 Bh3.** The combinative process arises quite naturally from Black's superior, effective and concentrated development.

20.Rd1. Or 20.Rg1 Bg2+; 21.Rxg2 Re1+. **20...Bg2+; 21.Kg1 Bxf3+; 22.Kf1 Bg2+.** Missing the more speedy 22...Rg2. (23.d4 Rxh2!) 23.Qd3 Rxf2+; 24.Kg1 Rg2+, followed by ...Rg1# — Steinitz. **23.Kg1 Bh3+.** Quicker is 23...Be4+; 24.Kf1 Bf5; 25.Qe2 Bh3+; 26.Ke1 Rg1# — Maroczy.

24.Kh1 Bxf2; 25.Qf1 Bxf1; 26.Rxf1 Re2; 27.Ra1 Rh6; 28.d4 Be3. In many ways an undistinguished game, both before and after the sacrifice, but Morphy's splendid conception on move 17 redeems all. **0–1.**

(3) MORPHY - AMATEUR
New Orleans, 1858

Morphy was particularly devastating against amateur players, which should not come as any surprise. Sooner or later, less experienced players tend to play a positionally unsound move, and then the master can exploit that to win quickly. In the following game, the amateur plays well for a while, but then falls down at a critical moment.

1.e4 e5; 2.Nf3 Nc6; 3.Bc4 Bc5; 4.b4 Bxb4; 5.c3 Ba5; 6.d4 exd4; 7.0-0 dxc3; 8.Ba3 d6; 9.Qb3 Nh6; 10.Nxc3 Bxc3?!; 11.Qxc3 0-0; 12.Rad1 Ng4; 13.h3 Nge5; 14.Nxe5 Nxe5; 15.Be2.

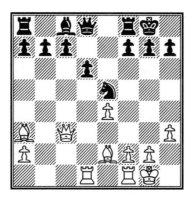

15...f5? An atrocious positional blunder which weakens the diagonals towards his king. With his opponent in possession of the bishop-pair he should have closed the position with 15...f6. **16.f4 Nc6; 17.Bc4+ Kh8; 18.Bb2 Qe7; 19.Rde1 Rf6** to make way for the queen.

20.exf5 Qf8.

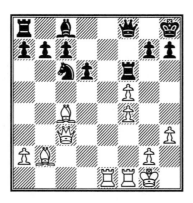

21.Re8! The conclusion devised by Morphy is dazzling, but not difficult to see or to calculate. **21...Qxe8; 22.Qxf6 Qe7; 23.Qxg7+.** Here Morphy could have crowned his combination with the simple 23.Qxe7 Nxe7; 24.f6. Instead he overcomplicates.

23...Qxg7; 24.f6.

24...Qxg2+. Not allowing Morphy the full glory of his magnificent, but somewhat unnecessary conception: 24...Qf8; 25.f7+ Ne5; 26.fxe5 h5; 27.e6+ Kh7; 28.Bd3+ Kh6; 29.Rf6+ Kg5; 30.Rg6+ Kf4; 31.Kf2 and mate by g2-g3, or Rg4 in the case of ...h4. **25.Kxg2 Bxh3+; 26.Kxh3 h5; 27.Rg1. Black resigned.**

(4) MORPHY - ANDERSSEN
Paris, 1858

The merit of Morphy's combination in the following game is enhanced, in our eyes, by the fact that his demolished opponent was a master of the very first rank. Nevertheless, (as in the game Kolisch-Anderssen) one must express surprise that Anderssen, an accomplished practitioner of the combinative vein, should succumb so rapidly to a direct sacrificial onslaught.**1.e4 c5; 2.d4 cxd4; 3.Nf3 Nc6; 4.Nxd4 e6; 5.Nb5 d6; 6.Bf4 e5; 7.Be3.**

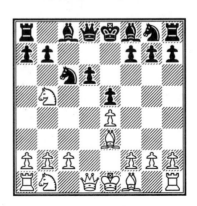

7...f5?! "To dare to embark on a counter-attack in such an exposed position is to challenge the logic of things," as Tartakover put it. Over a century later, the first game of the candidates match between Fischer and Petrosian, Buenos Aires, 1971, went 7...Nf6; 8.Bg5 Be6; 9.N1c3 a6; 10.Bxf6 gxf6; 11.Na3 d5!; 12.exd5 Bxa3; 13.bxa3 Qa5. Black obtained a good position, but later lost. Szen-Anderssen, 2nd game, London, 1851, saw yet another divergence: 7...a6; 8.N5c3 Be6; 9.Nd5 Bxd5; 10.Qxd5 Nf6; 11.Qb3 d5; 12.Qxb7 Nb4; 13.Na3 Nxe4 with sharp play from which Szen eventually won.

8.N1c3 f4. It is too late for 8...a6, e.g., 9.Nd5 axb5; 10.Bb6 followed by Nc7+ and the raider will escape.

9.Nd5! It would be too degrading for Morphy to retreat, although the positional 9.Bc1 is by no means bad, since Black has already wrecked his own pawn-structure. The combination launched by the text does, however, possess the merit of being absolutely sound.

9...fxe3; 10.Nbc7+ Kf7. 10...Kd7 loses to 11.Qg4#!

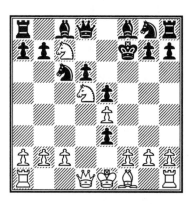

11.Qf3+?! This cavalier continuation is actually less convincing than 11.Nxa8 exf2+; 12.Kxf2 Qh4+; 13.g3 Qxe4; 14.Bg2, etc.

11...Nf6; 12.Bc4 Nd4. The only defensive possibility. To insert 12...exf2+; 13.Qxf2 would deprive Black of this useful tempo and leave him without resource against the discovered check.

13.Nxf6+ d5!; 14.Bxd5+.

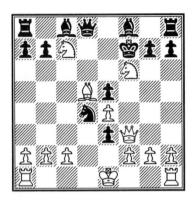

14...Kg6? Overlooking the possibility of a fresh sacrifice. Black could try to struggle on in an ending with 14...Qxd5; 15.Nfxd5+ Nxf3+; 16.gxf3 exf2+; 17.Kxf2 Bc5+; 18.Ke2 Rb8, but the best move is 14...Ke7! when White, indeed, has a powerful attack, but also a bewildering number of pieces en prise. After 14...Ke7! there is a long forced line analysed out by Zukertort and Maroczy: 15.Qh5 gxf6; 16.Qf7+ Kd6; 17.Nxa8 Nxc2+; 18.Ke2 Qe7. (18...Nxa1; 19.Bxb7 Nc2; 20.fxe3! and 21.Rd1+. But they overlook 20...Nd4!, as pointed out by Vinay Bhat. Therefore, White should play 19.Rc1!). 19.Qxe7+ Bxe7; 20.Rac1 Nd4+; 21.Kxe3 Bd7; 22.Rc7 Rxa8; 23.Rxb7. Here Zukertort and Maroczy give 23...Bc6, which is absurdly passive. Much stronger is (23...Rc8! threatening ...Rc2 and ...f5, which surely merits an assessment of unclear.)

How much of this did Morphy see? We suspect very little, since the records reveal that he took less than 30 minutes for the whole game! In that case should he be censured for "missing" 11. Nxa8? To this we must oppose Lasker's remark that Morphy was an artist, not a butcher, and in the mid-nineteenth century butchery had not yet become a necessity for the chess master. In 1858 one did not lose rating points if one's brilliant combination turned out to be not quite sound.

15.Qh5+! Kxf6; 16.fxe3 Nxc2+. Premature desperation, although Black still loses after 16...Qxc7; 17.exd4! Bb4+; 18.c3 Bxc3+; 19.Ke2 Ke7; 20.Rhf1. **17.Ke2.** Black resigned here, in view of 17...Qxc7; 18.Rhf1+ Ke7; 19.Rf7+ Kd6; 20.Rxc7 Kxc7; 21.Rc1, etc.

(5) MORPHY - DUKE OF BRUNSWICK & COUNT ISOUARD
Paris Opera House, 1858

This is one of the most famous games in the literature, played at the Paris Opera. While the fat lady was singing onstage, Morphy was bringing his own little opera to a close with a stirring finale!
1.e4 e5; 2.Nf3 d6.

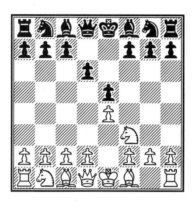

3.d4 Bg4. This is no longer played. The preferred plans today are a capture at d4, or a solid position with ...Nd7. **4.dxe5 Bxf3?** Black's best chance is to make a gambit of necessity with 4...Nd7! **5.Qxf3 dxe5.** The problem with this position, for Black, is that White has the bishop pair, a long-term asset. **6.Bc4 Nf6; 7.Qb3 Qe7.**

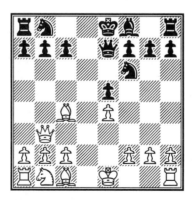

8.Nc3. If 8.Qxb7, then Black can escape into a (lost) ending with 8...Qb4+. Given the circumstances of the game, Morphy just didn't feel like capturing the pawn at b7. That would have taken the fun out of the game and deprived us of an imperishable jewel of chessboard imagination.

8...c6; 9.Bg5 b5.

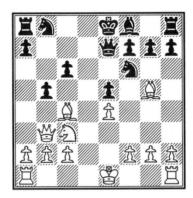

10.Nxb5! That's more like it. Morphy sacrifices a knight for the b-pawn, instead of capturing it for free at his eighth turn. **10...cxb5.** The noble amateurs chivalrously accept everything, but 10...Qb4+; 11.Qxb4 Bxb4+; 12.c3! is quickly decisive. **11.Bxb5+ Nbd7.**

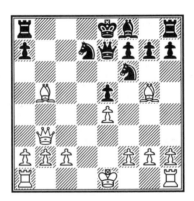

12.0-0-0 Rd8. Both knights are pinned, and Morphy now trades one pin for another. **13.Rxd7 Rxd7; 14.Rd1 Qe6; 15.Bxd7+ Nxd7.** Black has an extra piece, but White checkmates in two moves. **16.Qb8+! Nxb8; 17.Rd8#.**

(6) MORPHY - LOEWENTHAL
London, 1859

Morphy's opponent in this game was one of the best known players and theoreticians of the mid-19th century. He contributed many interesting new ideas in the opening, but his experiments often got him into trouble, too. Here a seemingly solid opening plan gets crushed by Morphy, who takes advantage of the only open pathway to the Black king.

1.e4 e5; 2.Nf3 Nc6; 3.Bc4 Bc5; 4.b4 Bxb4; 5.c3 Bc5; 6.0–0 d6; 7.d4 exd4; 8.cxd4 Bb6; 9.d5 Ne5; 10.Nxe5 dxe5; 11.Bb2 Qe7?; 12.Bb5+.

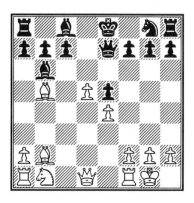

12...Bd7?; 13.Bxd7+ Kxd7; 14.Qg4+ f5; 15.Qxf5+ Ke8; 16.Bxe5. Black's resistance has been deplorable and he might well have resigned here.

16...Nh6; 17.Qf4 Kd7; 18.Nd2 Rae8; 19.Nc4 Bc5; 20.Rad1 Bd6; 21.Bxd6 cxd6; 22.Rb1 b6; 23.Rfc1 Qf6; 24.Qe3 Ng4.

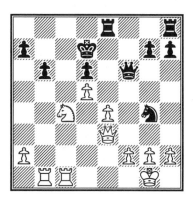

25.Nxb6+. Very pretty, but it is only a little extra icing on a cake long since baked. **25...axb6; 26.Rc7+ Kd8.** Or 26...Kxc7; 27.Qxb6+ Kd7; 28.Qa7+ Kd8; 29.Rb8#. **27.Qxb6 Qxf2+; 28.Qxf2 Nxf2; 29.Ra7! Nh3+; 30.gxh3 Kc8; 31.Kf2. Black resigned.**

FIND THE WIN!

(1) DE RIVIERE - MORPHY
Paris, 1863

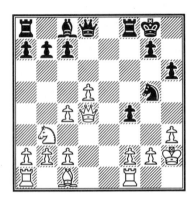

Black's pieces seem too far away to cause any problems, but Morphy manages to rip open the position. How?

(2) MARACHE - MORPHY
USA, 1857

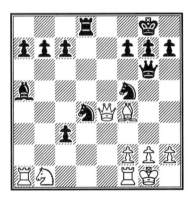

Black's pieces are starting to converge on the White king, and the passed c-pawn is a great asset. All that is irrelevant, really, because there is a quick kill. What is it?

(3) MORPHY - DE RIVIERE
Paris, 1858

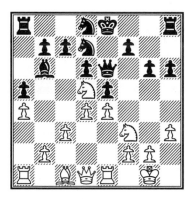

Morphy does not fail to notice that the enemy queen has no place to run. How did he exploit it?

(4) MORPHY - MONGREDIEN
Paris, 1859

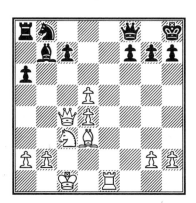

The back rank is weak. How does Morphy use a combination to exploit it?

4. WILHELM STEINITZ

First Official World Champion (1886–1894)

Of all the World Champions, Steinitz has generally been the most neglected when it comes to the art of combinative play. A firm believer that victory is best achieved through the accumulation of small advantages, and one of the best defenders of his day, Steinitz advanced the technical foundations of chess strategy, but was not generally inclined to flashy play. Nevertheless, he rarely failed to employ a combination when the opportunity presented itself. Many of his games show both artistic creativity and instructional displays of combinational skill.

Despite the great number of impressive combinations brought off by Steinitz, his sacrificial play somehow lacks the charismatic luster of Morphy's. Possibly his combinations exhibited excessive conformity to a strategic theme; for example, his mastery of an assault on the wing given a closed center was complete. Steinitz regarded himself as the first great publicist of defensive and positional principles. In the combinational sphere we might look upon him as the pioneer of "consolidation in attack."

Steinitz's own attitude is revealed in the following passage from his *Modern Chess Instructor*: "even the sound combinations that involve great sacrifices very rarely present difficulties as great as the maintenance of the balance of the position, and the strategy required in leading up to the final winning process." It is much harder to play good positional chess, he maintains, than to spot a brilliant combination. He wrongly predicted that brilliancies would become so commonplace as to be trivial, and scoffed at the idea that large prizes should be offered for the most brilliant game in each tournament, as was often the case until rather recently.

Well, that was Steinitz's view in his mature years. Almost a quarter century before he won his World Championship match, he was pounding out combinations that are still admired today. Let's take a look at a few.

(7) STEINITZ - MONGREDIEN
London, 1862

Mongredien was fan of extravagant and eccentric openings, which sometimes led to a very bad position early in the game. He was not a very skilled defender either. It is not surprising that he fell prey to numerous combinations! Steinitz exploits his opponent's inferior play to establish a strong position.

1.e4 d5; 2.exd5 Qxd5; 3.Nc3 Qd8; 4.d4 e6; 5.Nf3 Nf6; 6.Bd3 Be7; 7.0–0 0–0; 8.Be3 b6; 9.Ne5 Bb7; 10.f4 Nbd7; 11.Qe2 Nd5; 12.Nxd5 exd5; 13.Rf3.

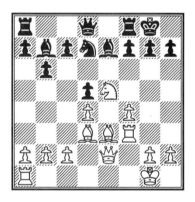

Threatening 14.Bxh7+ Kxh7; 15. Rh3+ Kg8; 16.Qh5 and **White wins. 13...f5; 14.Rh3 g6; 15.g4 fxg4; 16.Rxh7! Nxe5.** 16...Kxh7; 17.Qxg4 is just a transposition. **17.fxe5 Kxh7; 18.Qxg4 Rg8; 19.Qh5+ Kg7; 20.Qh6+ Kf7; 21.Qh7+ Ke6; 22.Qh3+ Kf7; 23.Rf1+ Ke8; 24.Qe6.** The two quiet moves, during the conduct of the attack, enhance the quality of Steinitz's conception. After the text, Black's king has no escape. **24...Rg7; 25.Bg5 Qd7; 26.Bxg6+ Rxg6; 27.Qxg6+ Kd8; 28.Rf8+. Black resigned**, as it is mate in one.

(8) DUBOIS - STEINITZ
London, 1862

In this game we see how murky the definition of a combination is. Although the latter portion of the game does contain a minor tactical finesse, it is in the opening that the truly deep sacrifice takes place. Black's 8th move invites White to win a lot of material. Old analysis of the combination is very superficial. It is likely that Steinitz had considered most of the main ideas seen in the analysis we present. We will never know, however, and thus the analyst's reluctance to enter into the most complicated lines perhaps robs Steinitz of an even larger slice of immortality.

1.e4 e5; 2.Nf3 Nc6; 3.Bc4 Bc5; 4.0-0 Nf6; 5.d3 d6; 6.Bg5 h6; 7.Bh4 g5; 8.Bg3 h5.

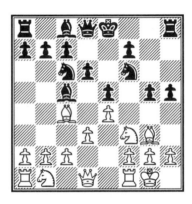

Did Steinitz know what he might have gotten himself into with this move? The complications are enormous, as we shall see, building on some long-published analysis and adding a bit of our own.

9.h4. We must diverge from the game to consider a spectacular combinational possibility.

9.Nxg5 is a sideline, not the actual game. The main line of the analysis is attributed to Loewenthal, but it may well have represented the likely continuation. In the 19th century, one was socially encouraged to accept sacrifices. To decline would be dishonorable, unless the acceptance of the sacrifice would lead to an almost immediate demise. Suicide was also dishonorable, and even illegal! So White would likely have grabbed the pawn at g5, even though ...h4 traps the bishop. After all, the pawn at f7 would fall with a fork against queen and rook.

9...h4 introduces some wonderful tactics. Whether it qualifies as a combination is unclear. Black sacrifices the queen for a strong attack on the enemy king.

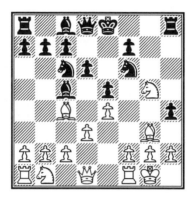

10.Nxf7 is now played. Black should reply 10...hxg3! after 11.Nxd8 Bg4; 12.Qd2 loses to 12...Nd4; 13.Nc3 (13.Bf7+ just delays the inevitable) 13...Nf3+; 14.gxf3 Bxf3; 15.hxg3 Rh1#. 11.Nxh8 is less greedy, though the ethics of the game at the time more or less required White to accept the offer of the queen. How does Black continue? Probably with 11...Bxf2+; 12.Kh1 Qe7, which transposes below to the next diagram. 12.Kh1.

Less effective is 10...Qe7; 11.Nxh8 hxg3; 12.Kh1! (12.Bf7+ is met by 12...Kd8; 13.Nd2 Bxf2+; 14.Kh1 Ng4; 15.Nf3 Qf6 and Black wins, according to Loewenthal, who also points out 12.Nf7 Bxf2+; 13.Rxf2 gxf2+; 14.Kxf2 Ng4+; 15.Kg3 Qf6; 16.Qf3 Qg7) 12...Bxf2 with an exciting position.

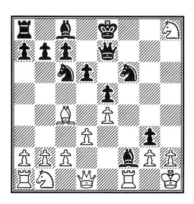

13.Bf7+ Kd8; 14.Nd2 (14.hxg3 Ng4; 15.Qd2 Qf6 wins a piece. 16.Ng6 Qxf7; 17.Qg5+ Ke8; 18.Qh5 Ne7; 19.Qh8+ Ng8. Black has a clear advantage) 14...Ng4; 15.Nf3 Qf6; 16.Qd2 Be3!

Back to the actual game, where more fireworks await us!

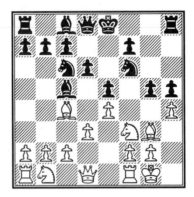

9...Bg4; 10.c3 Qd7; 11.d4. Now the center explodes. **11...exd4; 12.e5 dxe5; 13.Bxe5 Nxe5; 14.Nxe5 Qf5.**

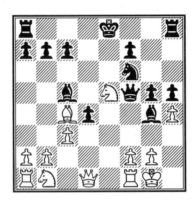

15.Nxg4. 15.Bxf7+ Kf8; 16.Qe1 is preferred by Loewenthal, but after 16...Bd6; 17.Nxg4 hxg4; 18.Qe6 Qxe6; 19.Bxe6 gxh4, Black is still much better. 20.cxd4 Re8; 21.Re1 h3; 22.Nc3 h2+; 23.Kh1 g3; 24.fxg3 Bxg3; 25.Re2 Kg7; 26.Rf1 Nh5; 27.Rf7+ Kg6; 28.Rf3 Bf4, and Black wins.

15...hxg4; 16.Bd3 Qd5; 17.b4 0–0–0!

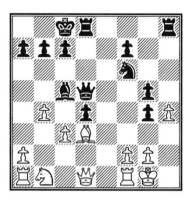

18.c4. 18.bxc5 Rxh4; 19.c6?? Rdh8! and White is quickly checkmated.

18...Qc6; 19.bxc5 Rxh4; 20.f3 Rdh8; 21.fxg4 Qe8; 22.Qe2.

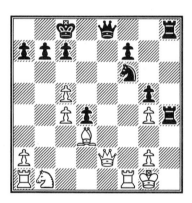

Black is down a piece, but forces victory by exchanging queens! **22...Qe3+!; 23.Qxe3.** Forced, or else it is mate at h1.

23...dxe3; 24.g3 Rh1+; 25.Kg2 R8h2+; 26.Kf3 Rxf1+; 27.Bxf1 Rf2+; 28.Kxe3 Rxf1.

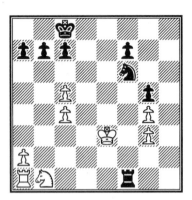

After all those exchanges, material is even, but White can already resign, because the pin on the knight at b1 cannot be broken, and the pawns are weak.

29.a4 Kd7; 30.Kd3 Nxg4; 31.Kc3. 31.Kc2 Ne3+; 32.Kd3 Nf5; 33.g4 Nh6; 34.Kc2 Nxg4 and the kingside pawns march forward. **31...Ne3; 32.Ra2.** Desperation, but Black was winning in any case. 32.Kd3 Nf5; 33.g4 Nh6 etc.

32...Rxb1; 33.Rd2+ Kc6; 34.Re2 Rc1+; 35.Kd2.

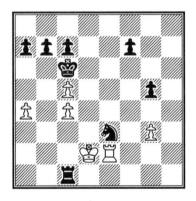

Has Black blundered? Not at all. The king and pawn endgame is a simple win. In this game, the accurate evaluation of the endgame led to an efficient win. **35...Rc2+!; 36.Kxe3 Rxe2+; 37.Kxe2 f5; 38.Ke3 Kxc5; 39.Kd3 f4. White resigned.**

(9) STEINITZ - MONGREDIEN
London, 1863

Our friend Mongredien is the victim once again. The double-fianchetto strategy is flawed. It is too slow. Steinitz puts the time to good use and develops quickly. His attack culminates in a fine combination.

1.e4 g6; 2.d4 Bg7; 3.c3 b6; 4.Be3 Bb7; 5.Nd2 d6; 6.Ngf3 e5; 7.dxe5 dxe5; 8.Bc4 Ne7; 9.Qe2 0-0; 10.h4. Inaugurating the classic Steinitz attack down the h-file. **10...Nd7; 11.h5 Nf6; 12.hxg6 Nxg6; 13.0-0-0 c5; 14.Ng5 a6.**

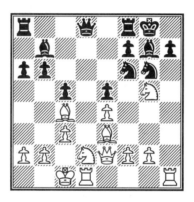

15.Nxh7! The unfortunate Mongredien falls victim to the self-same combination that struck him down one year previously. **15...Nxh7; 16.Rxh7 Kxh7; 17.Qh5+ Kg8; 18.Rh1 Re8; 19.Qxg6 Qf6; 20.Bxf7+!** The key to White's plot, which has effectively exploited both of the traditional weak points at h7 and f7. **20...Qxf7; 21.Rh8+ Kxh8; 22.Qxf7. Black resigns**, as 22...Rab8; 23.Qh5+ Kg8; 24.Qg6 is hopeless for Black. **1-0.**

(10) ZUKERTORT - STEINITZ
World Championship Match, 1886

This game was played in a contest for the title of World Champion, the first match to be officially recognized as a title contest. The best known combination from this match is the present game. The isolated d-pawn positions are known for their combinational opportunities, and the opening strategy was quite popular for Black at the time.

1.d4 d5; 2.c4 e6; 3.Nc3 Nf6; 4.e3 c5; 5.Nf3 Nc6; 6.a3 dxc4; 7.Bxc4 cxd4; 8.exd4 Be7; 9.0-0 0-0; 10.Be3 Bd7; 11.Qd3 Rc8; 12.Rac1 Qa5; 13.Ba2 Rfd8; 14.Rfe1 Be8; 15.Bb1 g6; 16.Qe2 Bf8; 17.Red1 Bg7.

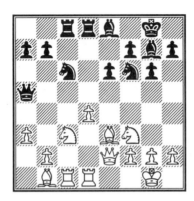

So far, play has followed in the typical fashion of an isolated d-pawn game. White attacks the kingside, Black tries to exploit the weakness of the d-pawn. The position is a Tarrasch Defense in reverse. **18.Ba2 Ne7; 19.Qd2.** White threatens a cheap tactic: Nd5!

19...Qa6; 20.Bg5 Nf5; 21.g4? This greatly weakens the kingside, and White will suffer for it in the end. White should have exchanged on f6 instead.

21...Nxd4!

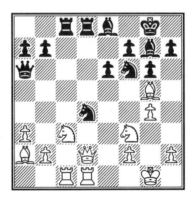

The sacrifice of the knight is only temporary.

22.Nxd4 e5; 23.Nd5 Rxc1; 24.Qxc1 exd4; 25.Rxd4 Nxd5.

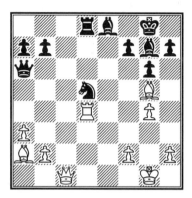

26.Rxd5. 26.Bxd8 Bxd4; 27.Bxd5 Qd6 picks off one of the bishops. **26...Rxd5; 27.Bxd5 Qe2; 28.h3 h6.** 28...Bxb2! was stronger, but Steinitz redeems himself in a few more moves. Yet, had he played this correct move, we never would have seen the concluding combination! Thus we again see that imperfection is sometimes required to achieve a combination.

29.Bc4 Qf3; 30.Qe3 Qd1+; 31.Kh2 Bc6; 32.Be7.

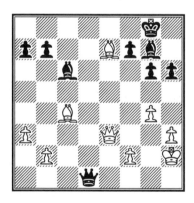

32...Be5+! A classic clean finish, offering a bishop to decoy the enemy queen to a square on which it will be vulnerable. **33.f4.** 33.Qxe5 Qh1+; 34.Kg3 Qg1+; 35.Kf4 (35.Kh4 Qxf2+; 36.Qg3 g5+; 37.Kh5 Qxg3; 38.Kxh6 Qh4#) 35...Qh2+ wins the queen. **33...Bxf4+; 34.Qxf4 Qh1+; 35.Kg3 Qg1+. White resigned.**

(11) STEINITZ - CHIGORIN
World Championship Match, 1892

As years went by, the Steinitzian attack slowed down a bit. In this game, we see a slow preparation for a brutal assault. This is truly a nasty form of the Spanish Inquisition, as even Chigorin, master of the Black side of the Spanish Game, finds to his discomfort.

1.e4 e5; 2.Nf3 Nc6; 3.Bb5 Nf6; 4.d3. The fashionable move now is 4.0-0, but there is nothing wrong with this quiet reinforcement of the center, and 4.Qe2, as suggested by the Spanish Inquisitor Ruy Lopez himself, is also well playable.

4...d6; 5.c3 g6. Instead of playing on the queenside with ...a6 ...b5, etc., Chigorin decides to operate along King's Indian lines. We should recall that Chigorin was the prophet of this defense.

6.Nbd2 Bg7.

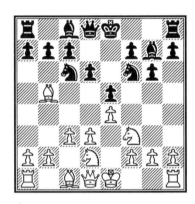

7.Nf1. Delayed castling–typical of Steinitz's profoundly cerebral approach to the Lopez. **7...0–0; 8.Ba4.** Preparing to come round to c2, from which square the bishop will reinforce White's center.

8...Nd7. Chigorin seems to be organizing the break ...f5, but this plan is faulty. He should either have left the f6-knight at its post and gone for immediate queenside expansion 8...a6; 9.Ne3 b5; 10.Bb3 Na5; 11.Bc2 c5, or else he should have met 9.Ne3 in the game continuation, with ...Nb6, trying to get in ...d6-d5. **9.Ne3 Nc5; 10.Bc2 Ne6; 11.h4!** The familiar Steinitz treatment.

11...Ne7; 12.h5 d5; 13.hxg6.

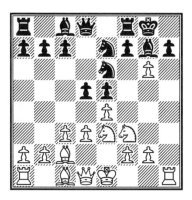

13...fxg6? A severe positional error (always capturing towards the center is one of the better "rules") in that Black irretrievably weakens the a2-g8 diagonal on which his king is situated. After 13...hxg6, White has nothing immediate. **14.exd5 Nxd5; 15.Nxd5 Qxd5; 16.Bb3 Qc6.** White controls two powerful open lines towards the Black king and, in view of Chigorin's lack of counterplay, it only remains for Steinitz to mobilize the remainder of his forces before the decisive attack will inevitably materialize.

17.Qe2 Bd7; 18.Be3 Kh8. A later World Champion, Max Euwe, commented: "He quits the line of the bishop but steps directly into the line of the rook." **19.0-0-0 Rae8; 20.Qf1.** A very fine move which prepares to open two new avenues of attack. **20...a5.** The wretched situation of Black's king leaves him curiously helpless to defend against the coming onslaught. **21.d4** with the threat of 22.d5, so Black has no choice.

21...exd4; 22.Nxd4.

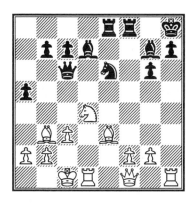

22...Bxd4. An invitation to disaster, but there is no defense, e.g. 22...Nxd4; 23.Rxh7+ Kxh7; 24.Qh1+ or 22...Qe4; 23.Bc2 Qg4; 24.f3 Qg3; 25.Nf5 gxf5; 26.Rxd7 and White wins. **23.Rxd4!** There are so many threats at this point (even the simple Rdh4 will be deadly) that Black may as well grab at the exchange.

23...Nxd4.

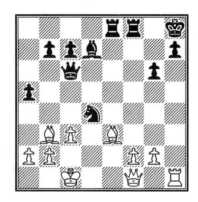

24.Rxh7+!! A beautiful denouement. Just as everyone was waiting for execution along the twin bishop diagonals Steinitz reveals his true plans with this stunning surprise. **24...Kxh7; 25.Qh1+.** A most original point of departure for a mating attack along the h-file. **25...Kg7; 26.Bh6+ Kf6; 27.Qh4+ Ke5; 28.Qxd4+ Kf5; 29.Qf4+.**

(12) STEINITZ - VON BARDELEBEN
Hastings, 1895

The most celebrated tournament of the 19th century took place in Hastings, England, in 1895. The Hastings tradition continues even to this day, and has produced more than its share of brilliancies. Steinitz helped bring the event fame with the following game, among the best known of his victories.

1.e4 e5; 2.Nf3 Nc6; 3.Bc4 Bc5; 4.c3 Nf6; 5.d4 exd4; 6.cxd4 Bb4+; 7.Nc3 d5?! Avoiding the complexities of 7...Nxe4!?; 8.0–0 Bxc3; 9.d5 which was unknown territory in 1895.

8.exd5 Nxd5; 9.0–0 Be6; 10.Bg5 Be7.

11.Bxd5. An unexpected exchange, the point of which is to delay Black's castling. **11...Bxd5; 12.Nxd5 Qxd5; 13.Bxe7 Nxe7; 14.Re1 f6; 15.Qe2 Qd7; 16.Rac1 c6?** Imperative was 16...Kf7! to break the pin. After the text Steinitz launches a combination which impoverishes adjectival description.

    17.d5! cxd5; 18.Nd4 Kf7; 19.Ne6 Rhc8; 20.Qg4 g6; 21.Ng5+ Ke8.

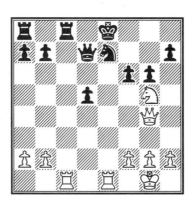

    22.Rxe7+! Kf8. The rook is immune, e.g. 22...Kxe7; 23.Re1+ Kd6; 24.Qb4+ Kc7; 25.Ne6+ Kb8; 26.Qf4+. But how is White to win with every piece en prise and Black threatening mate? **23.Rf7+! Kg8; 24.Rg7+! Black resigned.** Mate is forced: 24...Kh8; 25.Rxh7+ Kg8; 26.Rg7+ Kh8. (26...Kf8 loses to 27.Nh7+.) 27.Qh4+ Kxg7; 28.Qh7+ Kf8; 29.Qh8+ Ke7; 30.Qg7+ Ke8; 31.Qg8+ Ke7; 32.Qf7+ Kd8; 33.Qf8+ Qe8; 34.Nf7+ Kd7; 35.Qd6#.

FIND THE WIN!

(5) STEINITZ - SCOTT
Dundee, 1867

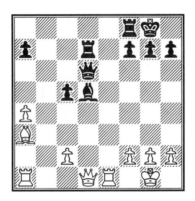

The lineup on the a3-f8 diagonal is the key here.

(6) STEINITZ - BLACKBURNE
London, 1876

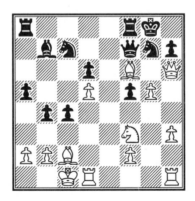

The goal here is to liberate the square White so desperately needs.

(7) STEINITZ - CHIGORIN
World Championship Match, Havana, 1892

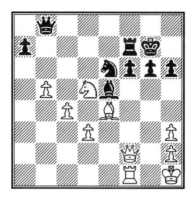

The Black king looks well defended, and White's chances appear to lie with his passed pawns. However, things are not what they seem.

(8) REINER - STEINITZ
Vienna, 1860

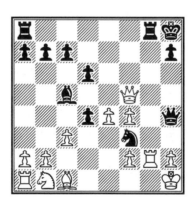

How does Black capitalize on the open files on the kingside?

5. EMANUEL LASKER

Second World Champion (1894–1921)

Lasker held on to the undisputed World Championship for over a quarter of a century, which is still a record. His tactical ability was matched by a creative faculty which, together, produced many fine games. His skill was such that he was usually able to win a game by purely technical means, but from time to time, a memorable combination also appeared on the chessboard.

Lasker had great confidence in his middlegame and endgame skills, and was not a deep strategist. He relied on his opponent to make an error at some point, and didn't worry about maintaining an opening advantage as White. His sense of danger was fantastic, and that same ability served him well in attack. His combinations often seem to spring out of thin air. Studying the complete games, which contain the combinations, will help you develop the sort of vision that lead Lasker to his greatest victories.

The quintessential genius Albert Einstein knew Lasker well. Lasker was rather critical of Einstein's 'Theory of Relativity', but that didn't carry over to personal relations. Indeed, Einstein wrote the foreword to Lasker's biography. "What he really yearned for was some scientific understanding and that beauty peculiar to the process of logical creation, a beauty from whose magic spell no one can escape who has ever felt its slightest influence." Lasker's combinations, as we shall see, show that beauty in a brilliant light.

(13) LASKER - BAUER
Amsterdam, 1889

This is, perhaps, the most celebrated of Lasker's brilliancies. It is typical of his style. A quiet opening settles into a meandering middlegame, where no clear stategy is displayed. The opponent's sense of danger is not sufficiently acute, and one positional mistake gives rise to one of the most memorable combinations. **1.f4 d5; 2.e3 Nf6; 3.b3 e6; 4.Bb2 Be7; 5.Bd3.** A crude move which limits White's strategic objectives to a kingside attack. Black's task over the next few moves should be to obliterate this bishop. A somewhat artificial move, but not entirely bad, because the c-pawn can advance to c4, and then the bishop can retreat to c2 or b1 as needed.

5...b6; 6.Nf3 Bb7; 7.Nc3 Nbd7; 8.0-0 0-0. Black has a solid position and White has no real advantage. **9.Ne2?!** Consistent with his plan of a kingside attack, but Black should have replied with 9...Nc5!, neutralizing White's powerful light square bishop. His failure to do this results in a rapid deterioration of his prospects.

9...c5; 10.Ng3 Qc7.

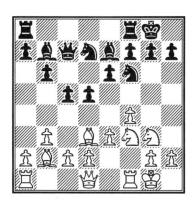

11.Ne5. White occupies this square before the Black pawn advances to e5. **11...Nxe5.** This also falls in too readily with White's plans—he should have tried 11...d4!? to break the diagonal of White's b2 bishop. With just one move, Black invites disaster. Moving one of the rooks to c8 would have been better.

12.Bxe5 Qc6; 13.Qe2 a6. White has completed development and is ready to attack. The position of the rook at a1 cannot be improved, for the moment. Lasker starts by eliminating one of the few defenders of the Black king, but he doesn't part with Be5.

14.Nh5 Nxh5. Unwittingly allowing the "double-bishop" combination. On the other hand, 14...Ne8 also loses spectacularly to 15.Bxg7!!

15.Bxh7+! Kxh7; 16.Qxh5+ Kg8.

17.Bxg7! This threatens mate at h8. **17...Kxg7.** Or 17...f6; 18.Rf3 Qe8; 19.Qh6 and **White wins**. **18.Qg4+ Kh7.** Now the queen guards g2 and White can threaten the sideways equivalent of a back rank mate. **19.Rf3 e5.** There is no recourse other than shedding the queen, but Lasker picks up a stray bishop as well. Now at least the Black queen can come to h6. **20.Rh3+ Qh6; 21.Rxh6+ Kxh6.**

22.Qd7. The final point of the combination. Black should have stopped here and the final moves are not so interesting. This wins one of the bishops, and the game now is decisively in White's favor.

22...Bf6; 23.Qxb7 Kg7; 24.Rf1 Rab8; 25.Qd7 Rfd8; 26.Qg4+ Kf8; 27.fxe5 Bg7. 27...Bxe5; 28.Qh5 f6; 29.Qxe5 shows another method of exploiting the pin on the f-file. **28.e6 Rb7; 29.Qg6.** White exploits the pin in the maximally efficient way. **29...f6; 30.Rxf6+ Bxf6; 31.Qxf6+ Ke8; 32.Qh8+ Ke7; 33.Qg7+. Black resigns.** An impressive tactical display.

(14) PILLSBURY - LASKER
Saint Petersburg, 1896

1.d4 d5; 2.c4 e6; 3.Nc3 Nf6; 4.Nf3 c5; 5.Bg5 cxd4; 6.Qxd4 Nc6; 7.Qh4?! Stronger is **7.Bxf6!**, as Pillsbury later discovered. **7...Be7; 8.0-0-0 Qa5; 9.e3 Bd7; 10.Kb1 h6; 11.cxd5 exd5; 12.Nd4 0-0; 13.Bxf6 Bxf6; 14.Qh5 Nxd4; 15.exd4 Be6; 16.f4 Rac8; 17.f5.**

Here Black invests an exchange to expose the enemy king. **17...Rxc3!; 18.fxe6.** By continuing with his counterattack, Pillsbury forces Lasker to reveal the full depth of his combination, for the game could have come to an abrupt and unspectacular conclusion after 18.bxc3 Qxc3; 19.fxe6 Rc8–winning. What is often overlooked is that the loser of a brilliant game can deserve credit for offering resistance that demands the highest quality of attack. **18...Ra3!!** A move that comes into the miraculous class. Since the a2-pawn is indefensible, Pillsbury is forced to accept.

19.exf7+ Rxf7; 20.bxa3 Qb6+.

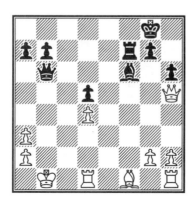

21.Bb5. 21.Kc2 also loses: 21...Rc7+; 22.Kd2 Qxd4+; 23.Ke1 Qc3+ etc. **21...Qxb5+; 22.Ka1 Rc7; 23.Rd2 Rc4; 24.Rhd1 Rc3.** Treading the same path as its former colleague. **25.Qf5 Qc4; 26.Kb2.**

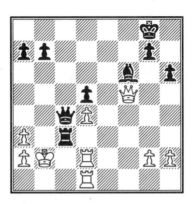

The combinations are not over yet! **26...Rxa3!!; 27.Qe6+.** If White takes the rook, then Black mates even quicker with 27...Qc3+; 28.Ka4 b5+!; 29.Kxb5 Qc4+; 30.Ka5 Bd8#. **27...Kh7; 28.Kxa3 Qc3+; 29.Ka4 b5+!; 30.Kxb5 Qc4+; 31.Ka5 Bd8+. Black resigned.**

(15) PORGES - LASKER
Nuremberg, 1896

Lasker's games show a great deal of patience, and for this reason brilliant combinations are not as common as in the case of other World Champions. Lasker was content to get a good position and build it, exploiting the opponent's mistakes ruthlessly and efficiently. In this example, nothing much happens at the start of the game. **1.e4 e5; 2.Nf3 Nc6; 3.Bb5 Nf6; 4.0-0 Nxe4; 5.d4 Be7; 6.Qe2 Nd6; 7.Bxc6 bxc6; 8.dxe5 Nb7.** Black's queenside looks strange.

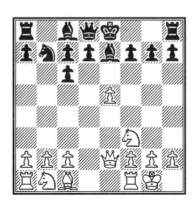

Nevertheless, White has no way to take advantage of it, and soon the pieces take up more natural posts. **9.b3.** Porges tries a move that Lasker himself introduced! **9...0-0; 10.Bb2 d5; 11.exd6 cxd6; 12.Nbd2 Re8; 13.Rfe1 Bd7; 14.Ne4 d5; 15.Ned2.** Lasker has achieved the first goal in the opening as Black-equality. Now he acquires a positional advantage by force.

15...Ba3!

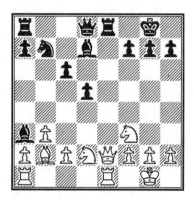

The White queen at e2 is attacked by the Black rook, so White's reply is forced. **16.Be5 f6; 17.Qa6 fxe5; 18.Qxa3 e4.** Black has the initiative and White has no defensive forces except the knight at f3, which is under attack.

19.Nd4 Qf6; 20.c3. This is necessary to support the knight, but it creates a major weakness which can be exploited later. **20...Rf8; 21.f3.** Lasker keeps forcing his opponent to make weakening defensive moves. **21...Qg5; 22.Qc1 Nc5; 23.Nf1 Qg6!** Of course Lasker will not exchange queens, he is on the attack!

24.Re3 Nd3; 25.Qd1 Nf4; 26.Ng3 h5; 27.Nde2.

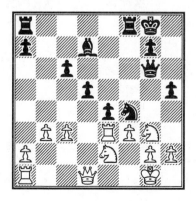

Lasker has prepared the attack well, and now uses a combination to finish off his opponent. **27...Nxg2.** This removes one of the main defenders of the king. Since the rook at e3 is attacked, Black's reply is forced. **28.Kxg2 exf3+; 29.Rxf3.** 29.Kh1 fxe2; 30.Qxe2 Bg4 and Black has a extra pawn, the initiative, and a continuing attack. **29...Bh3+.** Now if the king retreats, the rook at f3 falls.

30.Kxh3. 30.Kf2 Rxf3+; 31.Kxf3 h4 wins back the piece with no loss of power in the attack. After 32.Kf2 (32.Nh1 Qe4+; 33.Kf2. Black mates in 6 with 33...Rf8+; 34.Ke1 Qe3!; 35.Nhg3, meeting the threat of ...Rf1+, 35...hxg3; 36.Qxd5+ cxd5; 37.Kd1 Rf1+; 38.Kc2 Qxe2#) 32...Rf8+; 33.Ke1 hxg3; 34.Nxg3 Bg4, white cannot avoid the loss of further material. Although this is not a "pure" combination, the initial investment has paid off quite nicely.

30...Qg4+; 31.Kg2 Qxf3+.

Here the White king commits suicide, but commentators have tended to ignore the fact that there is no immediate forced win if the king returns to the h-file.

32.Kg1. 32.Kh3 Qg4+; 33.Kg2 h4; 34.Nd4 Qxd1; 35.Rxd1 hxg3 and now instead of recapturing at g3, White could try to hang on with 36.Nxc6, but after 36...gxh2; 37.Ne7+ Kf7; 38.Nxd5 Rh8, Black should win in the end. **32...h4; 33.Nh1 Qe3+. White resigned.**

(16) KAN - LASKER
Moscow, 1935

Although Lasker was not a prolific creator of combinations, he loved complex tactics that required calculation. His ability to see deeper than his opponents led to many victories, and even the passing of years did not dull his faculties, as this game shows.

1.d4 d5; 2.c4 c6; 3.cxd5 cxd5; 4.Nc3 Nc6; 5.Nf3 Nf6; 6.Bf4 Bf5. The quiet symmetry of the Exchange Variation of the Slav does not always lead to boring encounters. **7.Qb3 Na5; 8.Qa4+ Bd7; 9.Qc2 Rc8.** Black already has the initiative, and White's queen foray is exposed as a waste of time.

10.e3 b5; 11.a3 e6; 12.Bd3 Be7; 13.Ne5 Nc4; 14.Qe2 0-0; 15.0-0 Be8. This is played to create room for a knight at d7.

16.Rac1 Nd7; 17.Nxc4 bxc4; 18.Bb1 f5. Although the pawn at e6 is weak, the bishop at b1 is even weaker. **19.f3 Nb6; 20.Bc2 Bd6; 21.Bxd6 Qxd6; 22.Rcd1 Bd7; 23.Qd2 Bc6; 24.Rfe1 Rcd8; 25.Re2 Rd7; 26.Rde1 g6; 27.Rd1 Rb8; 28.Qe1 Rdb7.** It is part of Lasker's genius that he was able to prepare attacks well in advance. Here he sets up control of the b-file, which will play a critical role in the eventual combination. This is not really a deep strategic conception. Lasker simply puts his pieces on potentially useful squares.

29.Rdd2 Nd7; 30.Bb1 e5; 31.Qg3 Qe6; 32.e4 exd4; 33.exf5 Qf6; 34.Re6.

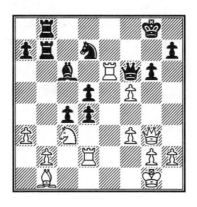

Lasker's queen is attacked, but, to the suprise of his opponent, he sacrifices it as part of a combination. **34...dxc3!!; 35.Rxf6 cxd2; 36.Rxg6+.** White has no choice. 36.Bc2 Nxf6; 37.fxg6 Rxb2; 38.gxh7+ Kh8; 39.Qe5 Rb1+!; 40.Kf2 Rf8! White's feeling hopeless. For example: 41.Qd6 Nxh7; 42.Qh6 d1N+!!; 43.Kg1 Nc3; 44.Bxb1 Nxb1; 45.Qxc6 Nc3. **36...hxg6; 37.Qxg6+ Kf8; 38.Qd6+ Ke8.**

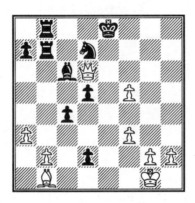

It is now clear that White cannot arrange a perpetual check. Materially, White has a queen and two pawns for two rooks and a knight, which is not a great difference. We must take into account, however, that Black's powerful pawn at d2 and the threats on the b-pawn add up to a decisive advantage, and White's four connected, passed pawns offer no relief.

39.Bc2. White has dual threats of f6 and Qxc6, but Black is prepared. **39...Rb6!; 40.f6 Kd8!; 41.f7 Kc8!** White is allowed to promote the f-pawn and win a piece, but Black can afford such sacrifices. **42.f8Q+ Nxf8; 43.Qxf8+ Kb7.** White has balanced the material, but the end is near. **44.Qf6 Ka6!; 45.Qd6 Re8!** Now Black will be able to advance the d-pawn and win back the piece. **46.h4 Re1+; 47.Kh2 Rc1; 48.Bf5.** Desperation. 48.Qg6 Ba4! wraps things up. **48...d1Q; 49.Bc8+ Ka5!** A remarkable journey by the Black king is a striking characteristic of this game. **White resigned** here.

(17) CHIGORIN - LASKER
London, 1899

This game features the relatively rare situation where both sides have castled on the queenside. This does not stop Lasker from launching an attack down the a-file, and he finishes with a pretty combination.

1.e4 e6; 2.Qe2. Chigorin's patent, which has the aim of preventing the typical advance 2...d5, since on 3.exd5 Black cannot recapture with the pawn. **2...Nc6; 3.Nc3 e5.** A very strange plan. Lasker figures that the queen is badly placed on e2, in the Vienna Game (1.e4 e5; 2.Nc3 Nc6), and that the extra tempo is irrelevant.

4.g3 Nf6; 5.Bg2 Bc5; 6.d3 d6; 7.Bg5 h6; 8.Bxf6 Qxf6; 9.Nd5 Qd8; 10.c3.

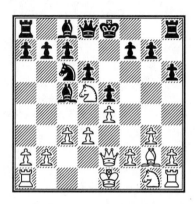

Chigorin has steered the game from a French to a Vienna which has worked out pretty well for him, though there is also nothing wrong with Lasker's position. It is easy to see that if Black castles on the kingside, White will go the other way and throw a barrage of pawns at the Black king, so Lasker decides to swing his king to the queenside.

10...Ne7; 11.Nxe7 Qxe7; 12.0-0-0 Bd7; 13.f4 0-0-0; 14.Nf3 Bb6; 15.Rhf1 f6; 16.Kb1 Rde8; 17.f5 Ba4; 18.Rc1 Kb8. Lasker has the bishop pair, but the position is closed so it is not of much value. The players dance for a while before getting down to business.

19.Nd2 a6; 20.Bf3 Ba7; 21.h4 Rc8; 22.Nc4 Rhd8; 23.Ne3 Be8; 24.Rfd1 Bf7; 25.c4 c6; 26.Rc2 Bd4. Black finally has one piece in an active position, but more support is needed before the attack can be launched.

27.Rdc1 Qc7; 28.Nd1 Qa5; 29.Nc3 b5! Now things open up. **30.b3 Rd7; 31.cxb5 axb5; 32.Nd5.** White takes advantage of the pin on the c-file to infiltrate, but accomplishes very little in the process.

32...Kb7; 33.g4 Rdd8; 34.Ne7.

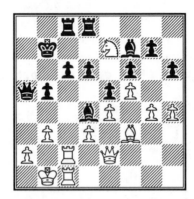

Now the tactics start to fly! Black doesn't care about the rook at c8, which wasn't doing anything anyway. Lasker's eyes are focused intently on the enemy king. **34...Bxb3!** Of course the bishop is taboo because of ...Qa1 mate. **35.Nxc8 Rxc8; 36.Qd2.** White was probably expecting Black to capture at c2, but instead, Lasker increases the pressure since the rook isn't going anywhere.

36...Qa3; 37.Rh1 Ra8; 38.Rh2.

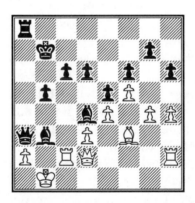

Of course Lasker could just take the rook at c2 here, so there was no need for an elegant combination, but mindful of the spectators Lasker provided a clever combination to finish the game. **38...Bxa2+!; 39.Rxa2 Qb3+; 40.Kc1.** 40.Rb2 Bxb2; 41.Qxb2 Qxd3+; 42.Rc2 Qxf3 is obviously hopeless for White. **40...Rxa2; 41.Qxa2 Be3+.** This is the key move, that was not so easy to see at the start of the combination, whose effect was to make this possible. **42.Qd2 Qxd3.** Chigorin had seen enough and **resigned**.

(18) LEE - LASKER
London, 1899

Here is another example of a patient buildup to a fine combination. Lasker plays a traditional Spanish game, resolves the central situation at move 18, and then improves the position to the point where a combination presents itself.

1.e4 e5; 2.Nf3 Nc6; 3.Bb5 a6; 4.Ba4 Nf6; 5.d3 d6; 6.c3 b5; 7.Bc2 g6; 8.a4 Bb7; 9.Nbd2 Bg7; 10.Nf1 d5. White's quiet play allows this active continuation. **11.Qe2 0–0; 12.Ng3 Qd6; 13.0–0 Rfe8; 14.h3 Na5; 15.Bd2 c5; 16.Rfd1 Qc7; 17.Qe1 c4; 18.d4.** Black's queenside initiative is growing, and White decides it is time to force matters in the center.

18...Nxe4; 19.Nxe4 dxe4; 20.Nxe5 Bxe5; 21.dxe5 Qxe5.

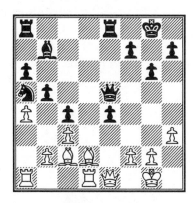

As a result of the exchanges, Black has several advantages, including a permanent control of more space, a great deal of influence at d3, and in the long term, attacking possibilities. Black is up a pawn. The attack will require the assistance of the bishop at b7, so White blockades the e-pawn.

22.Be3 Nc6; 23.b3 Na5; 24.b4 Nc6; 25.Rd7. Usually one fears the invasion of the seventh rank, but there White has no supporting forces and the 7th can be defended laterally.

25...Re7; 26.Rdd1 Rd8; 27.Rxd8+ Nxd8; 28.axb5 axb5; 29.Qd2 Ne6; 30.h4 Bc6; 31.Ra6 Rd7; 32.Qe1 Bb7; 33.Ra5. The rook does not accomplish much at a5. **33...f5; 34.g3.**

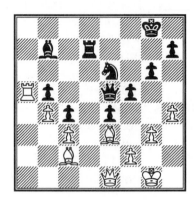

Now the strategy of the attack takes place. The goal is to get the bishop at e3 to move, advance the e-pawn, and use the open lines to converge on the enemy king. **34...f4!; 35.gxf4 Nxf4; 36.Bd4?** Lee fails to appreciate that the bishop at e3 is holding his game together, though one must admit that the position was already pretty bad. 36.Bxf4 Qxf4; 37.Qe3 Qxe3; 38.fxe3 was ugly, but necessary.

36...Qf5; 37.Qe3.

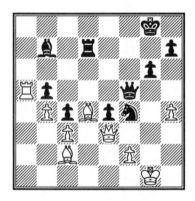

It looks as though White is keeping the position closed, but a combination by Lasker exposes the weaknesses. **37...Rxd4!; 38.cxd4 Qg4+; 39.Kf1 Qg2+; 40.Ke1 Qg1+; 41.Kd2.** Now what? It looks as though the enemy king has escaped, and the bishop at b7 remains a spectator. **41...c3+!; 42.Qxc3.** 42.Kxc3?? loses to 42...Nd5+.

42...Qxf2+; 43.Kd1. 43.Kc1 Ne2+ is terminal. **43...e3.** Now there is a threat of ...Bf3+ and the e-pawn is edging closer to the promotion square. **44.Bb3+ Kg7; 45.d5+.** This cuts off the bishop. **45...Kh6; 46.Qe1 Bc8! White resigned**, as the bishop will enter via g4.

FIND THE WIN!

(9) LASKER - STEINITZ,
World Championship (2nd Game), 1896

Lasker got off to a good start in his title defense, with a crushing sacrifice against Steinitz's king. Where is the mating attack?

(10) JANOWSKI - LASKER
Paris, 1909

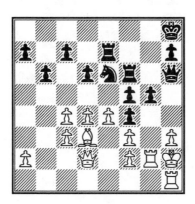

How does Black break through?

(11) LASKER - PIRC
Moscow, 1935

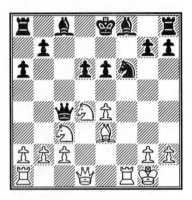

White to move. Black's position has a glaring weakness. That is the key to solving this position.

(12) LASKER - FORBES-ROBERTSON
Cheltenham, 1898

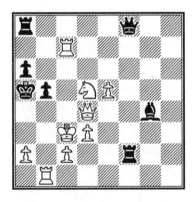

White is very close to checkmating the enemy king, but what is the most efficient kill?

6. JOSE RAUL CAPABLANCA

Third World Champion (1921-1927)

Capablanca was one of the most accurate of World Champions. He rarely blundered either tactically or strategically. He could see the hidden mines of the battlefield at a glance, and played very rapidly. His ability to avoid mistakes brought him great success, both in tournament and match play. Sooner or later his opponents would find a way to give the Cuban Grandmaster an opportunity to gain the advantage, and Capablanca would take it.

Capablanca, in his *Last Lectures*, wrote that combinations are so varied and so numerous, that it isn't possible to give any general advice. Yet in his games, he rarely failed to find the brilliancies when the position was ripe. As Réti once said of Capablanca, "in a sense, chess is his mother tongue." Here we will examine some of his poetry. Learn his language well and it will help you in your games.

(19) RÉTI - CAPABLANCA
Berlin, 1928.

Would Réti himself have included this game in a revision of his classic *Masters of the Chessboard*? Unfortunately, his premature death in 1929 left that question unanswered. The high praise heaped on Capablanca in that book would have been fully justified by the play in this game.

1.e4 e5; 2.Nf3 Nc6; 3.Bb5 d6; 4.c3 a6; 5.Ba4 f5; 6.d4. Modern theory indicates that 6.exf5 Bxf5; 7.0-0 Bd3; 8.Re1 Be7; 9.Bc2 gives White an edge. **6...fxe4; 7.Ng5 exd4; 8.Nxe4 Nf6; 9.Bg5 Be7; 10.Qxd4.** White miscalculates and Black won't be able to take advantage of the exposed queen. **10...b5.** Winning material, but White

must have felt that so many pawn moves would allow counterplay.
11.Nxf6+ gxf6; 12.Qd5 bxa4.

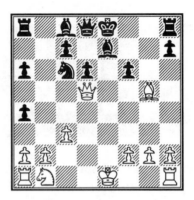

13.Bh6. 13.Qxc6+ achieves nothing against 13...Bd7. **13...Qd7; 14.0-0 Bb7.** Aiming his extra piece straight at White's king position. **15.Bg7 0-0-0.** Another fine move. Black has no choice but to give back a little material to take the initiative. After White takes the rook, Black will have his queen bishop, knight, queen and rook all aiming at White's king, which has no defenders. **16.Bxh8 Ne5.** Now White's queen won't be able to get back to defend the kingside.
17.Qd1.

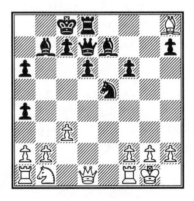

17...Bf3. Very powerful. Black wins a tempo on White's queen, while not allowing any counterplay. The sacrifice must be accepted, or else ...Qh3 is an easy win. **18.gxf3.** 18.Qd4 Qh3; 19.gxh3 Rg8+; mates. **18...Qh3.** White has no defense to threats like 19...Nxf3+ and 19...Rg8+, so Réti **resigned**.

(20) CAPABLANCA - HAVASI
Budapest, 1928

Capablanca has suffered some adverse press in that his public image is often projected as that of a colorless, risk-free technician. But, we wonder how many people realize that a sharp sacrificial idea, normally associated with Keres and Tal, was actually pioneered by Capablanca?

1.d4 d5; 2.c4 e6; 3.Nf3 dxc4. This move was considered bad for a long time, but has recently been resurrected in Grandmaster circles. **4.e4.** This was the proper reaction for many years, but now it is considered harmless. Such players as World Championship Candidates Korchnoi and Hübner, and rising star Rublevsky, played it in 1997, with positive results. **4...c5.** Today's preference is 4...b5, but the text is still seen, from those who don't know their history!

5.Bxc4 cxd4; 6.Nxd4 Nf6; 7.Nc3.

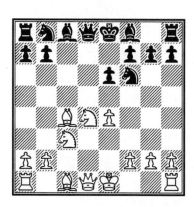

7...a6? Even worse than 7...Bc5 which Bogoljubow essayed against Capablanca at Moscow, 1925. The sequel was 8.Be3 Nbd7; 9.Bxe6! (according to Golombek, Capablanca played the sacrifice immediately) 9...fxe6; 10.Nxe6 Qa5; 11.0–0 Bxe3; 12.fxe3 Kf7; 13.Qb3 Kg6; 14.Rf5 Qb6; 15.Nf4+ Kh6 and now Capablanca would have won outright with 16.Qf7! Instead he played 16.g4? but still won after various complications.

8.0–0 Bc5; 9.Be3 Nbd7.

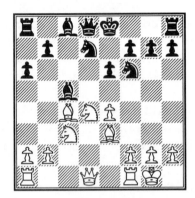

9...0-0 was the only chance, for the text permits Capablanca to unleash his combination with added punch. **10.Bxe6!** Capablanca also brought off a similar sacrifice in his game against Mieses at Margate 1935. 1.d4 d5; 2.c4 c6; 3.Nf3 Nf6; 4.e3 e6; 5.Nc3 Nbd7; 6.Bd3 dxc4; 7.Bxc4 a6; 8.e4 c5; 9.e5 Ng4; 10.Ng5 Nh6; 11.Bxe6! and White won, since 11...fxe6 fails to. 12.Nxe6 Qa5; 13.Bd2 cxd4; 14.Nd5! wins.

10...fxe6; 11.Nxe6 Qa5; 12.Nxg7+ Kf7.

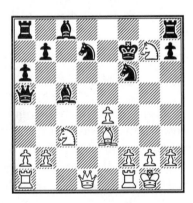

13.Nf5. In addition to his three pawns worth of material compensation, White is aided by the exposed position of Black's knight and his inability to co-ordinate his other pieces. Meanwhile, Capablanca's mobilization proceeds apace. **13...Ne5; 14.Qb3+ Kg6; 15.Rac1 Bf8.** A very odd move, but 15...Bxe3; 16.fxe3 would let White's f1–rook into the game, very much as in the Bogoljubow game. **16.Ne2 h5; 17.Rfd1 Rg8; 18.Nf4+ Kh7.**

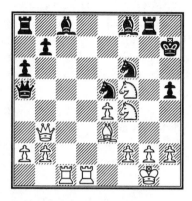

19.Bb6 Qb5; 20.Rc7+ Kh8. Or 20...Bg7; 21.Qxg8+ Kxg8; 22.Rxg7+ Kf8; 23.Rd8+ Ne8; 24.Rxc8 and White wins. **21.Qxb5!** The final link in the combination. It is typical of Capablanca's lucid style to not avoid the queen exchange, but he had to see a very fine point on move 24. **21...axb5; 22.Rd8 Rxa2; 23.Rdxc8.**

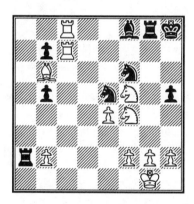

23...Nc4. Does Black regain the piece? **24.h3! Nxb6; 25.Rxf8 Nfd7.** Or 25...Rxf8; 26.Ng6+ Kg8; 27.Nh6#. **26.Rf7 Rxb2; 27.Nd5. Black resigned.**

(21) ALATORTSEV - CAPABLANCA
Moscow, 1935

The following game is a gem from Capablanca's last years as an active player, but it is often left out of anthologies of his best games. A classic exploitation of an open file combined with a weak back rank makes this one of his instructive, and purest, combinations.

1.d4 Nf6; 2.c4 e6; 3.Nc3 d5; 4.Bg5 Be7; 5.e3 0-0; 6.cxd5 Nxd5; 7.Bxe7 Qxe7; 8.Nf3 Nxc3; 9.bxc3 b6; 10.Be2 Bb7; 11.0-0 c5; 12.Ne5. White's whole plan in this game is to trade as many pieces as possible, as quickly as possible, in hopes of making an early draw.

12...Nc6; 13.Nxc6 Bxc6; 14.Bf3 Rac8; 15.a4 cxd4; 16.cxd4 g6; 17.Bxc6 Rxc6; 18.Qd3 Qb7; 19.Rfb1 Rfc8; 20.h3 a6; 21.Qa3. Just as White is almost within sight of his draw haven, he starts to play badly. Here 21.Rb2 defends adequately since Black's control of the c-file is balanced by White's pressure against the queenside pawns.

21...Rc2. White must now try 22.Rc1. **22.Qd6?**

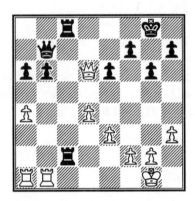

The final error, although it takes play of very high order to exploit it. It is easy to see that the focus of Black's operations lies at g2, where the scope of the powerful queen at b7 and rook at c2 converge. What is not so obvious is how to make it work, but Capablanca unleashes a powerful combination that reduces White's position to rubble. **22...Rxf2!!; 23.Qg3.** The sacrifice cannot be accepted: 23.Kxf2 Rc2+; 24.Kg3 Qxg2+; 25.Kh4 (25.Kf4 Rf2+; 26.Ke5 Rf5#) 25...g5+; 26.Kh5 Qxh3+; 27.Kxg5 Rg2+; 28.Kf6 Qh4+; 29.Ke5 Rg5+; 30.Kf6 Rh5+. **23...Rcc2.** Unfortunately for White, it is clear that the sacrifice cannot be declined. **White resigned.**

(22) MARSHALL - CAPABLANCA
New York, 1931

Combinations overlooked by world champions are relatively rare but can be just as revealing as those that they play. The following game contains a devastating trick overlooked by both Capablanca and the resourceful American Grandmaster Frank Marshall. It has taken over half a century for the error to be discovered!

1.Nf3 Nf6; 2.d4 e6; 3.c4 b6; 4.g3 Bb7; 5.Bg2 Bb4+; 6.Bd2 Bxd2+; 7.Nbxd2. More aggressive is 7 Qxd2. **7...0–0; 8.0–0 c5; 9.dxc5 bxc5; 10.Rc1.** Again, more vigorous is 10.Qc2 as in the game Bogoljubow - Nimzowitsch, Berlin, 1927. **10...Qc7; 11.Nb3 d6; 12.Qd2 Nc6; 13.Rfd1 Rfd8; 14.Nh4 a5.** This energetic advance gives Black the advantage. **15.a4 Rab8; 16.Rc3 Ba8; 17.h3 Nb4; 18.Bxa8 Rxa8; 19.Qf4 Qc6; 20.Rf3 Rd7; 21.g4 Qxa4.** A premature harvest. By playing 21...Ra6, Black could have retained his attack against White's queenside, while strengthening his own center and avoiding any tactics. However, Capablanca has missed a trick.

22.Rxd6 Nbd5.

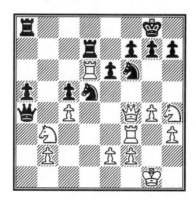

Capablanca's play is very clever since 23.cxd5 fails to 23...Qxf4; 24.Rxf4 Rxd6. Nevertheless both players, as well as all subsequent commentators failed to see that White has the magnificent resource here 23.Ra6!! The main line, discovered by Grandmaster John Nunn continues 23...Nxf4; 24 Rxa8+ Rd8; 25.Rxd8+ Ne8; 26.Rxf4 g5; 27.Rf3 gxh4; 28.Nxc5, with an easy win. **23.Qe5 Rxd6; 24.Qxd6 Ne4; 25.Qe5 Qxc4; 26.Rd3 a4; 27.f3 Nef6; 28.Nd2 Qc1+; 29.Kf2 h6; 30.f4 c4; 31.Rd4 c3; 32.bxc3 a3; 33.g5 a2; 34.Nb3 Qxc3; 35.gxf6 Qxb3; 36.Rd1 Qxd1.** White resigned.

(23) CAPABLANCA - SOUZA CAMPOS
Sao Paulo, 1927

Capablanca frequently punished inferior play in the opening. He was never thrown off by unorthodox strategies, and applied simple postional concepts to gain a significant advantage. Then he would sweep the powerless opponent off the board with a potent combination.

1.e4 b6; 2.d4 Bb7; 3.Bd3 e6; 4.Nf3 c5; 5.0–0 cxd4. Transposing into a very inferior version of the Sicilian Defense. **6.Nxd4 Ne7; 7.Nc3 Ng6; 8.Be3 Bc5; 9.Qh5 0–0; 10.Rad1 Bxd4; 11.Bxd4 Nc6; 12.Be3 e5.** Black's entire handling of the opening is disastrous. First he surrenders the bishop pair, and now he leaves himself with a horribly backward pawn in the d-file.

13.Bc4 Kh8; 14.Rd6 Qe7; 15.Rfd1 Rad8; 16.Bg5 f6.

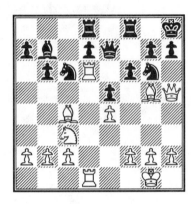

Black's opposition has been decidedly inferior, but Capablanca's exploitation of this is brilliant. **17.Qxg6 hxg6; 18.R6d3 Rf7; 19.Nd5 Qc5; 20.Rh3+ Kg8; 21.Nxf6+ Kf8.** 21...gxf6; 22.Bxf6 and mate cannot be avoided. **22.Rh8+ Ke7; 23.Re8+ Rxe8; 24.Rxd7+ Kf8; 25.Rxf7#.**

(24) CAPABLANCA - STEINER
Los Angeles, 1933

This was an exhibition game played with live pieces. The play was also very lively! Capablanca takes advantage of a structural weakness in the enemy position with brutal efficiency.

1.e4 e5; 2.Nf3 Nc6; 3.Nc3 Nf6; 4.Bb5 Bb4; 5.0–0 0–0; 6.d3 d6; 7.Bg5 Bxc3; 8.bxc3 Ne7. A weak move. Correct is 8...h6; 9.Bh4 Bg4 as in a game Capablanca - Lasker, St Petersburg, 1914.

9.Nh4. White's threat to play f4 forces Black into a sad weakening of his kingside pawn structure. **9...c6; 10.Bc4 Be6; 11.Bxf6 gxf6; 12.Bxe6 fxe6; 13.Qg4+.** After this astute check, Black's king is forced towards the center and White's onslaught runs on oiled wheels.

13...Kf7; 14.f4 Rg8; 15.Qh5+ Kg7; 16.fxe5 dxe5.

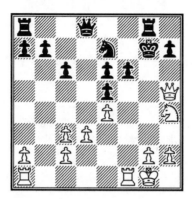

Given slow play by White, Black might still play ...Ng6 and survive. However, Capablanca strikes with a winning combination at just the right moment. **17.Rxf6 Kxf6; 18.Rf1+ Nf5; 19.Nxf5.** Absolutely precise. The more materialistic 19.exf5 would allow Black's king to flee to the queenside. **19...exf5; 20.Rxf5+ Ke7; 21.Qf7+ Kd6; 22.Rf6+ Kc5.** If 22...Qxf6; 23.Qxf6+ Kd7; 24.Qxe5 with an easy win. The text, though, allows White to finish with a magnificent flourish. **23.Qxb7 Qb6; 24.Rxc6+ Qxc6; 25.Qb4#.**

FIND THE WIN!

(13) CAPABLANCA - FONAROFF
New York, 1904

This is a famous example of Capablanca's tactical skill. Deliver crushing blows until the enemy must concede the game!

(14) CAPABLANCA - MIESES
Berlin, 1931

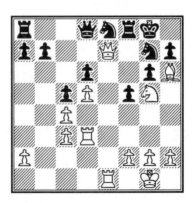

The kingside is a little congested. Clear up the situation with a combination!

(15) CAPABLANCA - YATES
Barcelona, 1929

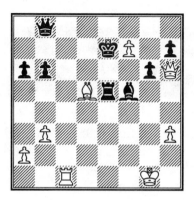

The Black queen is overworked. How can you exploit this?

(16) CAPABLANCA - LASKER
Berlin Speed Game, 1914

White to move. Do you know your endgames well enough to win this position?

7. ALEXANDER ALEKHINE

Fourth World Champion (1927–1935 and 1937–1946)

Alekhine is the most combinative of the World Champions. Tal may have been the magician of the sacrifice, and several could lay claim to superior tactical prowess, but Alekhine was a rare mix of attacking spirit and confident tactician. His games are always part of a chessplayer's education. He was a creative genius who trusted his intuition and let it carry him to the supremacy of the chess world for the better part of two decades.

The most instructive aspect of Alekhine's games is the way in which he builds up his position before undertaking any violent action. At times he did so in a completely original fashion, as in his experiments with the hypermodern 1.e4 Nf6, which has, since its debut, been known as the Alekhine Defense. Even in standard chess openings he aimed for a strategic undermining of the enemy position.

The dominance Alekhine held over his nearest rivals was so great that his superior play gave rise to more than his share of combinational possibilities. Only decades later would Bobby Fischer achieve a similar stature, a rare tradition being carried on, now by Garry Kasparov. We are fortunate in having such a large and instructive legacy to draw on.

(25) RÉTI - ALEKHINE
Baden-Baden, 1925

Alekhine considered this game to be one of the finest he ever played. It is a work of profound depth that Alekhine was able to handle Réti's radical new opening strategy. This is an achievement in itself, but the combination is astonishing. Yet there is a flaw, recently discovered by British Grandmaster John Nunn.

1.g3 e5; 2.Nf3 e4; 3.Nd4 d5; 4.d3 exd3; 5.Qxd3 Nf6; 6.Bg2 Bb4+; 7.Bd2 Bxd2+; 8.Nxd2 0–0; 9.c4 Na6. Alekhine has obtained nothing special from the opening, which makes his subsequent creation of a brilliant attack even more impressive.

10.cxd5 Nb4; 11.Qc4 Nbxd5; 12.N2b3 c6; 13.0–0 Re8; 14.Rfd1 Bg4; 15.Rd2 Qc8; 16.Nc5 Bh3; 17.Bf3 Bg4; 18.Bg2 Bh3; 19.Bf3 Bg4.

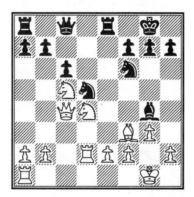

20.Bh1. 20.Bg2 would have been equal. **20...h5.** With this thrust did Alekhine already foresee his coup on move 26? **21.b4 a6; 22.Rc1 h4; 23.a4 hxg3; 24.hxg3 Qc7; 25.b5 axb5; 26.axb5.**

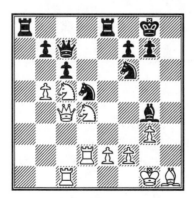

26...Re3!! Threatening ...Rxg3+ and 27.fxg3 Qxg3+ followed by ...Ne3 is obviously out of the question, but this is only the start of the combination which winds its intricate way for a further fourteen moves. Actually, as we shall see, this is more of a drawing combination than a winning combination, since White had resources, some of which were discovered only quite recently, that were overlooked in the game.

27.Nf3. Alekhine dismissed 27.Kh2 with 27...Raa3!; 28.fxe3 Nxe3 followed by ...Nf1+. Alekhine gives 27...Bxf3; 28.exf3 cbx5; 29.Nxb5 Qa5; 30.Rxd5 Re1+; 31.Rxe1 Qxe1+, but Jonn Nunn found 32.Kg2 Nxd5; 33.Qxd5 Ra1; 34.Qd8+ with a draw. This may reduce the sporting value of the combination, but does not detract from its artistic impression. In fact, if we consider the position after White's 26th move to be better for White, as would seem to be the case given the weakness of Black's pawns on the queenside, then the combination was not only justified, but perhaps necessary!

27...cxb5; 28.Qxb5 Nc3; 29.Qxb7 Qxb7; 30.Nxb7 Nxe2+; 31.Kh2 Ne4! With reduced material, Alekhine continues to find brilliant tactical solutions aimed at the capture of White's stray b7-knight.

32.Rc4.

32...Nxf2; 33.Bg2 Be6; 34.Rcc2 Ng4+; 35.Kh3 Ne5+; 36.Kh2 Rxf3; 37.Rxe2 Ng4+; 38.Kh3 Ne3+; 39.Kh2 Nxc2; 40.Bxf3 Nd4. White resigns. 41.Re3 Nxf3; 42.Rxf3 Bd5! wins. A sublime masterpiece, even if the combination should only have been good enough for a draw.

(26) ALEKHINE - RESHEVSKY
Kemeri, 1937

Perhaps indicating a sense of humor, Reshevsky adopts the defense named after his opponent! That doesn't prevent Alekhine from playing vigorously, and he challenges Black by sacrificing a pawn in the opening. Eventually the pawn must be returned, and Alekhine maintains his positional advantages and builds on them to create a fine combination.

1.e4 Nf6; 2.e5 Nd5; 3.Nf3 d6; 4.d4 Bg4; 5.c4. 5.Be2 is less risky. The text commits White to a pawn sacrifice, unless he prefers to release the central tension by exchanging on d6 at move six.

5...Nb6; 6.Be2!? dxe5; 7.Nxe5 Bxe2; 8.Qxe2 Qxd4; 9.0–0.

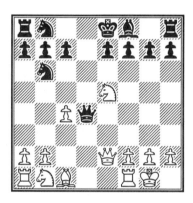

One of the most difficult operations to judge in chess is the soundness of a pawn sacrifice. When the opportunity arises to make a heavier material investment, it is normally obvious whether or not there will be a definite minimum compensation, but with the pawn sacrifice there is often a thin borderline between "good chances and "fizzling out." The feeling on these matters is extremely delicate and Alekhine was adept at finding precisely the correct moment for a pawn sacrifice to energize his own position.

9...N8d7; 10.Nxd7 Nxd7? An illogical move which Alekhine thoroughly castigated in his own notes, giving instead 10...Qxd7!; 11.a4 Qc6; 12.Na3 e6; 13.a5 Nd7; 14.Nb5. **11.Nc3 c6; 12.Be3 Qe5; 13.Rad1 e6; 14.Qf3 0-0-0.** White's lead in development made Black's position critical, hence Reshevsky's decision to return the pawn in the interests of decreasing the pressure.

15.Bxa7 Qa5; 16.Bd4 Qf5.

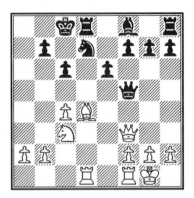

17.Qg3. 17.Qxf5 would have given White a good ending in view of his queenside pawn-majority, but as Alekhine put it: "The final attack of this game gave much more pleasure than a scientifically correct, but purely technical exploitation of a pawn majority on the queenside would do. After all, chess is not only knowledge and logic!"

17...e5; 18.Be3 Bb4; 19.Na4 Ba5; 20.f4 Bc7; 21.b3 f6; 22.fxe5 Qe6; 23.h3.

Here Alekhine has a note we like very much, a clear indication of his humorously realistic qualities as an annotator: "A good positional move which, however, is neither particularly deep nor difficult to find. Its main object is to prevent the possibility of ...Qg4 after 23...Nxe5; 24.Nc5, and also in some other variations the protection of white's g4 was essential. We were not a little surprised to read all the compliments addressed by the critics to the modest text-move, and also to the questioned–in all seriousness–after the game was over, whether by 23.h3 I already planned to play my queen to h2 on the 33rd move."

23...Rhg8; 24.Bd4 Nxe5; 25.Qc3.

25...Nd7. Covering the weak dark-square complex in the vicinity of his king. If 25...Kb8; 26.Nc5 Qd6; 27.Qb4 White is clearly better. **26.c5.** Nailing down the dark squares and also preparing a general advance of his queenside pawns against the Black king. **26...Rge8; 27.b4.** A second pawn sacrifice, but Black prefers to defer its acceptance. **27...Nb8.** Or 27...Qxa2; 28.Ra1 Qe6; 29.b5 and the Black king won't survive the opening of files on the queenside.

28.Nb6+ Bxb6; 29.cxb6 Qxa2; 30.Qg3 Rd7. If 30...Qf7; 31.Ra1! Rxd4; 32.Ra8 Re5; 33.Qxe5 and Black is busted. **31.Bc5.** Leading to a beautiful finish. Another neat conclusion would have been 31.Bxf6 gxf6; 32.Rxd7 Kxd7; 33.Qc7+ Ke6; 34.Re1+ and White wins.

31...Qf7; 32.Ra1 Qg6; 33.Qh2 Re5; 34.Ra8 Rd2.

Overlooking an enchanting combination, but if 34...Qe8; 35.Qg3! intending 36.Qa3 and **White wins. 35.Rxb8+! Kxb8; 36.Qxe5+! Black resigned,** because if the queen is captured, there is checkmate on the back rank.

(27) ALEKHINE - BOOK
Margate, 1938

This game has stood for many decades as a fine example of combinative play by Alekhine, who sacrifices a piece here. Is it really a combination? As things turn out, it is flawed, and we will see that Black missed a chance to survive. Should we therefore toss it out as having no value? Of course not. Although a sacrifice is different from a combination, in that a sacrifice may or may not force a material or positional gain, it is an important element of every combination.

We see here a sacrifice of a knight for the positional consideration of a double-pin against the bishop at d7. This is a useful pattern to remember.

1.d4 d5; 2.c4 dxc4; 3.Nf3 Nf6; 4.e3 e6; 5.Bxc4 c5; 6.0-0 a6; 7.Qe2 b5; 8.Bb3 Nc6; 9.Nc3 b4; 10.d5 Na5; 11.Ba4+ Bd7; 12.dxe6 fxe6; 13.Rd1!?

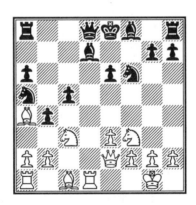

A complicated position. White not only offers a piece on c3, but follows with an exchange sacrifice at d7! **13...bxc3; 14.Rxd7 Nxd7; 15.Ne5 Ra7; 16.bxc3.** It was discovered some years later that Black may defend successfully here with 16...Qb8! as 17.Qh5+ offers White insufficient attack, and the attempt to recoup the material with 17.Nxd7 Rxd7; 18.Qxa6 fails to 18...Qd6! with the threat of ...Qd1+. 16.e4 might be a way of saving the combination because it gets the bishop at c1 into the game. What does Black do now against the threat of Qh5+? The plan with ...Qb8 does not seem to work. **16...Qb8.** (16...cxb2; 17.Bxb2 Qb6; 18.Rd1 is clearly better for White.) 17.Nxd7 Rxd7; 18.Qxa6, and here 18...Qd6 fails to 19.Qc8+! Ke7; 20.Bg5+! **16...Ke7?; 17.e4 Nf6; 18.Bg5 Qc7; 19.Bf4 Qb6.** 19...Qb7; 20.Qe3 Kd8; 21.Qd3+ Kc8; 22.Rb1 Qxe4 allows the brilliant finish 23.Nf7!! Qxd3; 24.Rb8#. **20.Rd1 g6; 21.Bg5 Bg7; 22.Nd7 Rxd7; 23.Rxd7+ Kf8; 24.Bxf6 Bxf6; 25.e5. Black resigned,** for if the bishop moves Qf3+ wins.

(28) ALEKHINE - KIENINGER
Poland, 1941

During the Second World War chess had to take a back seat to more serious matters, and very few international competitions were held. Alekhine managed to get by, by engaging in some actions and publications which have given rise to the question of his collaborations with the German side. This issue is complex, and best left to chess historians. It should be noted that before the war, Alekhine sent a letter of congratulations on the anniversary of the October Revolution, though he was certainly no communist. In any case, he did produce some sparkling chess before his death in 1946.

1.d4 Nf6; 2.c4 d6; 3.Nc3 e5; 4.Nf3 Nc6; 5.d5 Nb8; 6.e4 Be7; 7.h3 0–0; 8.Be3 Re8; 9.g4! c5; 10.Rg1 a6; 11.g5 Nfd7; 12.h4 Nf8; 13.h5.

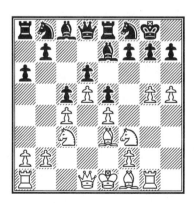

Black has just a single piece beyond the first rank, and that one is paralyzed with no available moves! **13...b6; 14.Nh4 g6; 15.Qf3 Ra7; 16.0–0–0 Qc7; 17.Bd3 Bd8; 18.Rg2 Kh8; 19.Rh1 Rb7.**

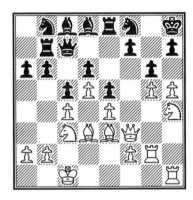

The way is prepared. Alekhine must have had difficulty not breaking out in a grin when looking at Black's wayward pieces. The only defender of consequence sits at g6. **20.Nf5!!** Alekhine sacrifices a knight just to get one pawn out of the way, but that pawn is the key to Black's defense. **20...gxf5.** 20...Kg8; 21.Nh6+ Kg7; 22.Rgh2 and Black is going to take a beating on the h-file.

21.exf5 e4. A desperate attempt to get some breathing room, hoping that the knight on b8 can find its way to e5. **22.Nxe4 Nbd7; 23.Bd2.** White is prepared for Black's jump to e5. The bishop will shift to c3, bearing down on the long diagonal and pinning the knight. So Black tries to close the diagonal down.

23...f6; 24.Bc3 Ne5.

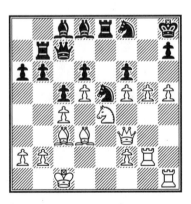

25.gxf6 Qf7. If Black had captured the queen, a nasty surprise would have been sprung by Alekhine: 25...Nxf3; 26.f7+ Ne5; 27.Rg8#. **26.Rhg1!!**

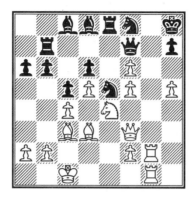

The queen is still taboo. **26...h6.** 26...Nxf3; 27.Rg8+ Qxg8; 28.f7+ Qg7; 29.Bxg7#. **27.Bxe5 Rxe5; 28.Rg7.** It is an easy win now. A beautiful example of combinative and attack play! **28...Qxg7; 29.fxg7+ Rxg7; 30.Rxg7 Kxg7; 31.f6+. Black resigned.**

(29) ALEKHINE - CAPABLANCA
AVRO, 1938

The AVRO tournament in Holland was one of the greatest tournaments of the period just before World War II. It featured the finest players of the day, and produced many excellent games. The contest between Alekhine and Capablanca was especially intriguing, and the players did not disappoint.

1.e4 e6; 2.d4 d5; 3.Nd2 Nf6; 4.e5 Nfd7; 5.Bd3 c5; 6.c3 Nc6; 7.Ne2 Qb6; 8.Nf3 cxd4; 9.cxd4 Bb4+; 10.Kf1. 10 Bd2 would allow Black to exchange queens by 10...Bxd2+; 11 Qxd2; Qb4. **10...Be7; 11.a3 Nf8; 12.b4 Bd7; 13.Be3 Nd8; 14.Nc3 a5; 15.Na4 Qa7; 16.b5 b6; 17.g3 f5; 18.Kg2 Nf7; 19.Qd2 h6; 20.h4 Nh7; 21.h5.**

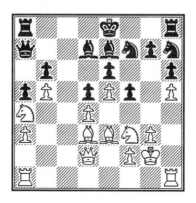

21...Nfg5. Better prospects of defense would be afforded by 21...0-0; 22.Nh4 Rfc8; 23.Ng6 Bd8 with the possibility, in some variations, of sacrificing the exchange by ...Rc4. Even so, by clearing the g-file, White would have a dangerous attack. The knight on g6 can hardly be ejected by ...Nh8 or ...Nf8 because White might leave it to be exchanged, subsequently sacrificing the bishop at h6.

22.Nh4 Ne4; 23.Qb2 Kf7; 24.f3 Neg5; 25.g4 fxg4; 26.Bg6+ Kg8; 27.f4 Nf3. If 27...Ne4, 28.Bxe4, and 29.Ng6 wins the exchange. 27...Nf7 is not immediately fatal, but White again removes the g-pawn and places his heavy pieces on the g-file. There is little Black can do to meet this threat. The combination is now launched.

28.Bxh7+ Rxh7; 29.Ng6 Bd8.

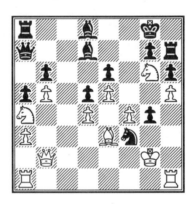

30.Rac1. This preparatory move is essential. If he goes for the knight at once by 30.Kg3 Rc8; 31.Kxg4 Rc4 and Black escapes; or 31.Rac1, again 31...Rc4 32.Rxc4 dxc4; 33.Kxg4 and the knight is not even threatened. **30...Be8; 31.Kg3 Qf7; 32.Kxg4 Nh4; 33.Nxh4 Qxh5+; 34.Kg3 Qf7; 35.Nf3 h5.** Before White could reply Black lost by overstepping the time limit. The position is, of course, hopelessly lost. A most unusual type of combination!

(30) ALEKHINE - FELDT
Tarnopol, 1916

Our last example of Alekhine's mastery is an early jewel, played during the First World War. It seems that, even with the entire world in an uproar, Alekhine was always able to keep focused on the combat at the chessboard. This combination is instructive because it involves a sacrifice on a bare square, which makes it all the more surprising.

1.e4 e6; 2.d4 d5; 3.Nc3 Nf6; 4.exd5 Nxd5. Unnecessarily complicating his opening task. 4...exd5 is more sensible. **5.Ne4 f5.** It is tempting to chase White's knight but the weaknesses left in the wake of this advance are too serious.

6.Ng5 Be7; 7.N5f3 c6; 8.Ne5 0–0; 9.Ngf3 b6; 10.Bd3 Bb7; 11.0–0 Re8; 12.c4 Nf6; 13.Bf4 Nbd7; 14.Qe2 c5.

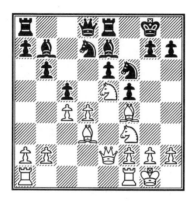

Black's position does not look so bad, but there are serious problems at f7 and e6 that Alekhine exposes in brutal fashion. **15.Nf7 Kxf7; 16.Qxe6+ Kg6.** 16...Kxe6; 17.Ng5#. **17.g4 Be4; 18.Nh4#.**

FIND THE WIN!

(17) ALEKHINE - EUWE
World Championship, 1937

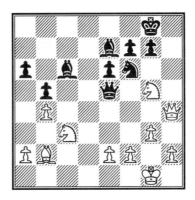

As with Capablanca, It is also revealing to observe when Alekhine, his great rival, exceptionally overlooked devastating combinations. Here, in a world championship game, Alekhine blithely defended his exposed pawn on b4. What should he have played?

(18) ALEKHINE - BOGOLJUBOW
Warsaw, 1941

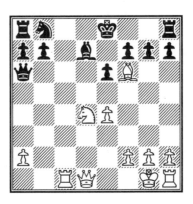

A strange situation where White is a pawn down, and has various units under attack. Black's development is in the fetal stage and White can exploit this to launch a blitzkrieg assault at first sight, though White may win with the prosaic 1.Bxg7 Rg8; 2.Bf6 Nc6; 3.Nxc6 Bxc6; 4.Qd6 nailing Black's head to the dark squares. But Bogoljubow had ingeniously prepared for this eventuality and would strike back with 4...Rxg2+; 5.Kxg2 Bxe4+, winning White's queen. Alekhine's solution is more effective and dramatic. Find it!

(19) ALEKHINE - FREEMAN
USA, 1924

Black's back rank is compeletely exposed. Alekhine found a way to bring the game to a rapid conclusion. What was it?

(20) ALEKHINE - OPOCENSKY
Paris, 1925

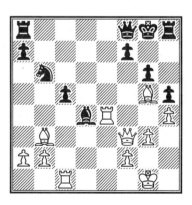

White has many targets on the kingside. One key square is g6, but it is not under attack yet. How can White open up the game and get to the target?

8. MAX EUWE

Fifth World Champion (1935–1937)

To some extent, Euwe is the Rodney Dangerfield of World Champions. He gets very little respect when compared to the giants such as Kasparov, Fischer, and even Alekhine, whom he dethroned in their 1937 match. Indeed, he is better remembered as a prolific author, and is, by far, the most published of the World Champions. His writings are considered among the best on the game, especially his treatises on the opening and the middlegame.

In his *Strategy and Tactics in Chess*, Euwe spent nearly the entire book on combinations. This makes sense, since combinations are the culmination of a good strategy combined with tactical accuracy. We very much like his description of the difference between combinative and normal situations: "For a short space of time special and not general rules apply; as it were an exceptional state of things prevails." He also was the first to divide the study of combinations into three tasks. First, the idea of the combination must be worked out. Then one must correctly evaluate the results of the combination. Of course the actual calculation of the variations is the third component.

Among all the World Champions, Euwe had the best ability to communicate the chess content of a game. His writings are superb. Yet we must not forget that he was also one of the greatest players of his time, and he has left us a number of beautiful combinations, including the following.

(31) EUWE - MAROCZY
Amsterdam (Match), 1921

An early game, in which Maroczy's unusual opening strategy leads to a position with a very strong center for White. The control of the center and great lead in development provides the positional basis for White's middlegame play, which leads to an opportunity for sacrificial and combinative play.**1.e4 e5; 2.f4 Bc5; 3.Nf3 d6; 4.c3 Bg4; 5.fxe5 dxe5; 6.Qa4+ Bd7; 7.Qc2 Qe7; 8.d4 exd4; 9.cxd4.**

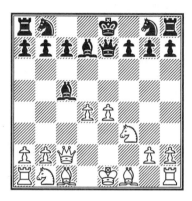

White's center has plenty of support, and the attack on the bishop gains time for development. **9...Bb4+; 10.Nc3 Bc6.** The attempt to use piece pressure to work against the strong center fails because since the king is still at e8, Black cannot effectively use a rook on the e-file. **11.Bd3 Bxc3+?** A serious miscalculation. Black needs to attend to development. Giving up this useful bishop for temporary custody of the e-pawn was misguided.

12.bxc3 Bxe4; 13.Bxe4 f5; 14.0-0! fxe4. Notice that Black's only developed piece is the queen! **15.Qb3!** The weakness of b7 is exposed. **15...c5; 16.Ba3 Nf6; 17.Bxc5.** Black just doesn't have time to take the knight.

17...Qf7; 18.c4 b6. 18...exf3; 19.Rae1+ Kd8; 20.Re7 Qxe7; 21.Bxe7+ Kxe7; 22.Qxb7+ Nbd7; 23.Qxf3 is an easy win for White.

19.Ng5 Qd7.

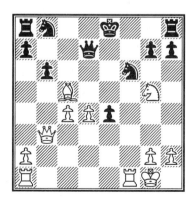

The knight at f6 is all that is holding Black's position together. White eliminates it with a combinative sacrifice. **20.Rxf6!! gxf6; 21.Nxe4.** The threat is now Nxf6+. **21...Qe6; 22.Re1,** re-establishing the threat, and now Black has no useful defense. **22...bxc5; 23.Nxf6+ Kf7; 24.Qb7+. Black resigned.**

(32) EUWE - ALEKHINE
Zurich, 1934

A clash of titans, which took place not long before the World Championship match saw the title move from Alekhine to Euwe. Alekhine adopts an unusual strategy in the Queen's Gambit Declined. Euwe, an opening theorétician for most of his life, gains a positional advantage which culminates in a combination.

1.c4 e6; 2.d4 d5; 3.Nc3 a6. Although this defense is playable, it neglects development somewhat and commits Black to an early move of his queenside pawns which may later prove inconvenient.

4.cxd5 exd5; 5.Bf4 Nf6; 6.e3 Bd6; 7.Bxd6 Qxd6; 8.Bd3 Nc6; 9.Nge2 0-0; 10.a3 Ne7; 11.Qc2 b6; 12.b4 Bb7. This bishop is now dead for some time. **13.0-0 Rfe8; 14.Ng3 Ng6; 15.Rfc1 Nh4; 16.Nce2 c6; 17.Rab1 Re7; 18.a4 Rae8; 19.a5.**

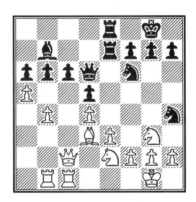

White's energetic advance forces weaknesses in Black's queenside. **19...b5; 20.Nf4 Rc7; 21.Qc5 Qd7; 22.Re1 Ng6; 23.Bf5 Qd8; 24.Nd3 Bc8.** Black finally prepares to rid himself of his inferior bishop, but White's initiative is growing apace. **25.Rbc1 Ne7; 26.Bxc8 Nxc8; 27.Ne5 Re6; 28.e4.** Alekhine was critical of this advance, since it turns a strategically overwhelming position into one based on tactics. Nevertheless, the tactics are of an exceptionally diabolical nature.

28...Nxe4; 29.Nxe4 dxe4; 30.Rxe4 f6.

31.Nf7!! An astounding move, occupying an empty square in the middle of the opponent's camp. Alekhine's previous move had been ...f6 which shows that he had either underestimated, or overlooked this coup.

31...Qe8. There is no choice. If 31...Rxf7; 32.Rxe6+ or 31...Kxf7; 32.Qh5+ Ke7. (32...g6; 33.Qxh7+ Kf8; 34.Qh8+ Ke7; 35.Rxe6+) 33.Rxe6+ Kxe6; 34.Re1+ and Black is mated.

32.Rxe6 Qxe6; 33.Nd8 Qe4; 34.Nxc6 h6.

35.d5. White has won an important pawn by means of his combination (the most scientific exploitation of f7 in this collection) and his position is now crushing.

35...Qd3; 36.h3 Qd2; 37.g3 Kh8; 38.Kg2 Qd3; 39.Re1 Kh7; 40.Re3 Qd2; 41.Re8 Qd3; 42.Qd4 Qc4; 43.Qe4+ Qxe4+; 44.Rxe4 Kg8; 45.Nb8 Kf7; 46.Nxa6 Rd7; 47.Rd4 Ne7; 48.d6 Nf5; 49.Rd5

Nxd6; 50.Nc5 Rd8; 51.Ne4 Nb7; 52.a6 Ke6; 53.Rxd8. Black resigned.

(33) GELLER - EUWE,
Zurich Candidates, 1953

The great tournament at Zurich 1953 is among the most famous in all of chess. The high quality of the games, annotated in the classic book by David Bronstein, led to breakthroughs in opening, middlegame and endgame strategy. One of many fine combinations from the event is seen in the following game.

1.d4 Nf6; 2.c4 e6; 3.Nc3 Bb4; 4.e3 c5; 5.a3. An aggressive variation of the Nimzo-Indian, and one that was extremely popular with Geller in the 50s, but we cannot help feeling that it is illogical to force Black into the doubling of White's c-pawns. We prefer 5.Bd3 or 5.Nge2.

5...Bxc3+; 6.bxc3 b6; 7.Bd3 Bb7; 8.f3 Nc6; 9.Ne2 0–0; 10.0–0.

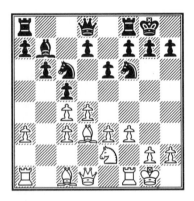

10...Na5. A good alternative is 10...Rc8. After the text, it is clear that Black will win White's front c-pawn, but at the cost of allowing a storm to burst over his king.

11.e4 Ne8. Capablanca's defensive maneuver designed to preempt the pin (Bg5). In addition Black prepares to blockade the advance of White's kingside pawns with either ...h6 or ...f5.

12.Ng3 cxd4; 13.cxd4 Rc8; 14.f4 Nxc4.

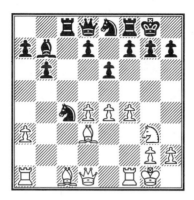

15.f5. Threatening the **pawn sacrifice** 16.f6! which would tear Black's kingside to shreds after ...Nxf6; 17.Bg5, etc. **15...f6!; 16.Rf4.** The attack against Black's h7-pawn introduced with this move looks decisive, but subsequent analysis revealed that White would have obtained value for the pawn with 16.a4 e5; 17.d5. Naturally, Geller could not be expected to appreciate this in over the board play, the more so since Euwe's defense is extremely refined.

16...b5; 17.Rh4 Qb6; 18.e5.

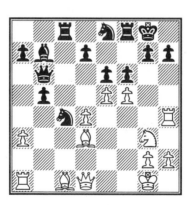

Black sees that the pawn at d4 is pinned on the diagonal and grabs the e-pawn.

18...Nxe5; 19.fxe6 Nxd3; 20.Qxd3.

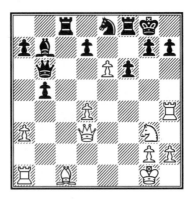

Quite feeble would be 20.exd7 Rxc1; 21.Rxc1 Nxc1; 22.dxe8Q Rxe8; 23.Qxc1. **20...Qxe6.** Here Black could, himself, fall victim to a combination: 20...g6; 21.Bh6 Ng7; 22.Bxg7 Kxg7; 23.Nf5+! gxf5; 24.Qxf5 Rh8; 25.Rg4+ Kf8; 26.Qxf6+.

21.Qxh7+ Kf7; 22.Bh6.

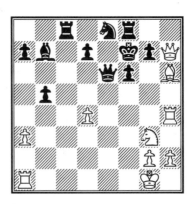

After 22.Qh5+ g6; 23.Qxb5, Black wins with 23...Rxc1+ and ...Qe3+. Geller must have felt rather confident at this point in view of the accumulation of threats against g7, but did Black's superior centralization leave him slightly suspicious?

22...Rh8!! A brilliant move, the key to Black's defensive combination. The point is to decoy White's queen from the protection of c2. Interestingly, Stahlberg (in the book of the tournament) gave 22...Rh8 a question mark since he could find no win for Black after 24.d5!

23.Qxh8 Rc2; 24.Rc1? Geller misses the best reply which was 24.d5! It seems that Euwe had played 22...Rh8!! more or less instinctively, since his own notes (written shortly after the game) gave only 24...Qb6+; 25.Kh1 Qf2; 26.Rg1 Bxd5; 27.Re4 Bxe4; 28.Nxe4 Qh4; 29.Nxf6 (29.Nd6+ Nxd6; 30.Qxg7+ Ke6; 31.Qg8+ Ke5; 32.Be3 Rc8; 33.Qg6 Nc4!-+) 29...Qxf6; 30.Be3 Qf5; 31.Bxa7 Ra2 with a clear advantage for Black. Or 24...Bxd5; 25.Rd1 Rxg2+; 26.Kf1 gxh6; 27.Qxh6 Ng7. However, the South African master Dreyer later published a deep analysis completely vindicating Euwe's decision: 24.d5 Qb6+; 25.Kh1 Qf2; 26.Rg1 Bxd5; 27.Re4 Bxe4; 28.Nxe4 Qh4. However White plays, he is in difficulties. **24...Rxg2+; 25.Kf1 Qb3; 26.Ke1 Qf3. White resigned.**

(34) KROONE - EUWE
Amsterdam, 1923

We go back in time to a fairly typical Sicilian from the 1920's. The Scheveningen Variation, named for a Dutch town where the opening made its first impact in the chess world, was very popular in Holland. Euwe shows a good understanding of the radical ideas that were quite new at the time.

1.e4 c5; 2.Nf3 Nc6; 3.d4 cxd4; 4.Nxd4 Nf6; 5.Nc3 d6; 6.Be2 e6; 7.0-0 Be7; 8.Be3 0-0; 9.Qd2 a6; 10.f4 Qc7; 11.Bf3 Na5; 12.Qf2 Nc4; 13.Bc1.

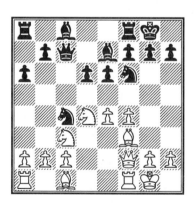

Euwe correctly judges the position and plays a powerful move in the center. **13...e5!; 14.fxe5 dxe5; 15.Nb3 Be6; 16.Kh1.** White is right to be careful. There is already a threat, for example: 16.h3 Nxb2!; 17.Bxb2 Bxb3! and if White captures the bishop, then ...Bc5

is terminal! This combination did not come to pass, but Euwe does not give up on the idea of the capture at b2.

16...Rfd8; 17.a4 Bb4; 18.Na2 Bf8!; 19.Qg3 Kh8; 20.Nc3 Rac8; 21.Nd1 Qc6; 22.Bg5? White is already suffering, and this move relieves the pain, only by shortening the game!

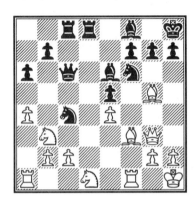

The stage is set. The tremendous pressure on the c- and d-file explodes in a fine combination. **22...Nxb2!; 23.Nxb2 Qxc2; 24.Bd1 Qxb2; 25.Rxf6 Qxa1!** 25...gxf6; 26.Bxf6+ is a trap that a player of Euwe's caliber was not likely to fall into. **White resigned.**

(35) EUWE - WEENINK
Amsterdam, 1923

Euwe was simply devastating in his hanlding of unusual openings, as we have already seen. There is enother example of a disreputable opening being ground into the dust and blown away by a big combination.

1.d4 f5; 2.e4. Euwe shows his aggression from the start by choosing the Staunton Gambit, but his opponent declines the offer and goes into the weak Balogh Defense, an unorthodox opening of almost no merit.

2...d6; 3.exf5! Bxf5; 4.Qf3 Qc8; 5.Bd3 Bxd3; 6.Qxd3. White is satisfied with the positional advantage which comes from the healthier pawn structure. Euwe builds on this advantage in a convincing manner.

6...Nc6; 7.Nf3 e6; 8.0-0 Qd7; 9.c4 0-0-0; 10.Re1.

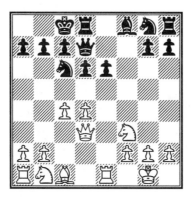

Pressure on the e-file keeps the Black forces tied down. **10...Nf6; 11.Bd2 Re8; 12.Na3 Be7; 13.b4 Rhf8; 14.b5 Nd8; 15.Nc2 Nh5!** Black wakes up to the danger and starts to create some counterplay on the kingside. **16.a4 g5!; 17.a5 g4; 18.Ng5 d5.**

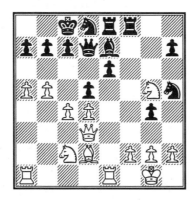

The time to attack is now! **19.b6! cxb6; 20.axb6 a6; 21.c5!** There is no stopping the White pawns. Black correctly exchanges at g5 to try to rescue some of the momentum. **21...Bxg5!; 22.Bxg5 Nc6.** What now? The queenside seems thoroughly blockaded. White has almost all pieces in position for a decisive breakthrough, but with a true master touch Euwe now brings the other rook into position. This quality of involving the maximum force in an attack is a hallmark of a strong Grandmaster. **23.Reb1! Qg7?** Black starts to crack under the pressure. 23...e5 was best, where White would have nothing better than capturing the pawn with a complicated position.

Attempts to win by brute force do not succeed, for example: 24.Rxa6 bxa6; 25.b7+ Kc7!; 26.Qxa6 Qf5 with counterplay against c2 and f2. **24.Be3 Kd7; 25.Nb4 Nxb4; 26.Rxb4 Rc8.**

The position seems sufficiently blockaded so that Black can survive even with a somewhat weak king. Yet, White breaks through with surprising ease, thanks to a combination.

27.Rxa6! bxa6; 28.b7 Rb8; 29.Qxa6.

As a result of this forced sequence White has a winning game. There are two main ideas at work here, the advance of the queenside pawns and direct threats against the enemy king. There is an additional resource, however, which Euwe does not fail to spot. The bishop at e3, seemingly asleep, can wake up to provide decisive pressure on the dark squares. **29...Qe7.** 29...Rfd8; 30.Qd6+ Ke8; 31.Qxe6+ Qe7; 32.Qg8+ Qf8; 33.Qxf8+ Kxf8; 34.c6 and the pawns are unstoppable. 29...Ke7; 30.Qd6+ Kf7; 31.c6 and the lady escorts the footsoldier to the queening square. **30.Bg5!** Another fine sacrifice, aimed at gaining control of d6.

   30...Qxg5; 31.Qd6+ Ke8; 32.Qxb8+ Kf7.

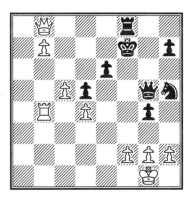

   Euwe does not miss the effective finish: **33.Qxf8+! Kxf8; 34.b8Q+. Black resigns.**

(36) EUWE - THOMAS
Hastings, 1934

   The game starts out as an English, but soon settles into a line in the Queen's Gambit Declined that was well known at the time, and in fact the first 17 moves were considered standard theory. Some combinations are cooked up at home, and then sprung on unsuspecting opponents at the board. This is one such case, Kasparov-Anand, which is presented later in the book, is another. **1.c4 e6; 2.Nc3 d5; 3.d4 Nf6; 4.Bg5 Be7; 5.e3 0-0; 6.Nf3 Nbd7; 7.Rc1 c6; 8.Bd3 dxc4; 9.Bxc4 Nd5; 10.Bxe7 Qxe7; 11.0-0 Nxc3; 12.Rxc3 e5; 13.Nxe5 Nxe5; 14.dxe5 Qxe5; 15.f4 Qe7; 16.f5! b5; 17.Bb3 b4.**

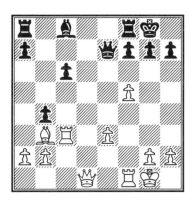

The importance of preparation was noted by Fred Reinfeld in his translation of Euwe's game collection, published as *From My Games (1920-1937)*. "...Euwe, some time before this game was played, set himself the problem of solving this particular variation, of determining whether White or Black or neither side had the better game after the opening moves. That this answer cannot possibly be refuted must be interpreted as meaning that the soul of the mathematician has spoken here." **18.f6!** With the rook at c3 under attack, this intermezzo came as a bit of a shock. **18...gxf6; 19.Rxc6 Qxe3+.** A meaningless pawn leaves the board. **20.Kh1 Bb7.**

It seems as though Black has some counterpressure on the diagonals, but his king is too exposed. **21.Rcxf6 Qe4; 22.Qd2! Kh8; 23.Bxf7 Rac8.** Black hopes to get this rook to c2. **24.R6f2! Rcd8?** A critical error, though after 24...Qg4 life was in any case unpleasant.

25.Qg5!! The queen takes up a powerful position and sets up the closing combination. 25.Bd5 is a theme we will see later, but right now it would lose because of the weakness of the back rank after 25...Rxf2!

25...Rd6.

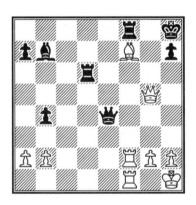

Some combinations are hard to see for purely optical reasons. The pattern of White and Black pieces here are so distinct that imagining White's next move is far from easy. **26.Bd5!! Black resigned,** as there was nothing left after 26...Bxd5. 26...Rxf2 loses to 27.Qg8#. **27.Rxf8+ Bg8; 28.Rxg8#.**

FIND THE WIN!

(21) EUWE - NAEGELI
Zurich, 1934

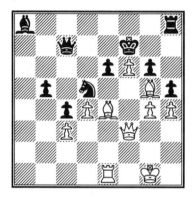

A classic case of switching between weaknesses–hitting one to get at another. Use all your pieces to achieve a winning position.

(22) EUWE - NESTLER
Dubrovnik, 1950

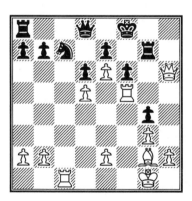

Can Black's carapace be cracked open?

(23) EUWE - ROSSETTO
Buenos Aires, 1947

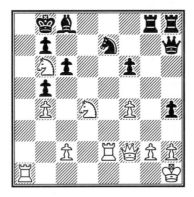

The Black king has very little room to roam, while the Black kingside threats are non-existent. Still, there is no reason to slow down the pace. On the contrary, heat it up and win quickly!

(24) TARRASCH - EUWE
Amsterdam, 1923

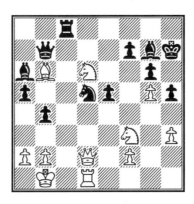

Black's forces are not directed at White's king, but they aren't sitting around twiddling their thumbs either. What devastating blow did Euwe unleash here?

9. MIKHAIL BOTVINNIK

Sixth World Champion (1948–1957, 1958–1960, and 1961–1963)

Botvinnik was the paragon of the Soviet School of Chess. He had balanced skills, was able to prepare important new opening strategies, handle both sharp and positional middlegames, and play efficiently in the middlegame. As effective in defense as on attack, he rose to the top of the chess world and stayed there for most of the post-war era.

The initiative was very important to Botvinnik, who loved to control the play whenever possible. Indeed, to the extent he could be beaten, it was usually through quiet positions where the great player seemed to become bored. Since he was at his best in active positions, it is not at all surprising that we see him as the father of many great combinations.

Botvinnik did not write a great deal about chess in general. He concentrated on collections of his own games, scrutinized carefully with constant revisions to previous analysis. In fact, Botvinnik claimed that all anyone needed to know about chess could be gleaned from studying his games. Luckily, this attitude has left a large collection of his games available to scholars and students. Here are just a few of his masterpieces.

(37) BOTVINNIK - CAPABLANCA
Avro, 1938

Beating Capablanca was an achievement that every World Champion in the first half of the 20th century achieved, and Botvinnik was the last of a long line to do so, though it was only ten years later he earned the title itself. Capablanca does not play badly, and it seems that his opening strategy leads to the win of a pawn. He underestimated Botvinnik's deep understanding of the position, and a combination puts an exclamation point on White's superior play.

1.d4 Nf6; 2.c4 e6; 3.Nc3 Bb4; 4.e3 d5; 5.a3 Bxc3+; 6.bxc3 c5; 7.cxd5 exd5; 8.Bd3 0-0; 9.Ne2 b6; 10.0-0 Ba6; 11.Bxa6 Nxa6; 12.Bb2 Qd7; 13.a4 Rfe8; 14.Qd3.

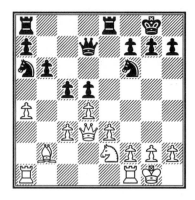

14...c4. This dooms White's a4-pawn, but leaves Botvinnik a free hand in the center.

15.Qc2 Nb8; 16.Rae1 Nc6; 17.Ng3 Na5; 18.f3 Nb3; 19.e4 Qxa4; 20.e5 Nd7; 21.Qf2 g6; 22.f4.

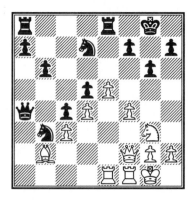

22...f5. Black is obliged to weaken himself in order to stem the avalanche. Blackburne faced the identical problem.

23.exf6 Nxf6; 24.f5! Rxe1; 25.Rxe1 Re8.

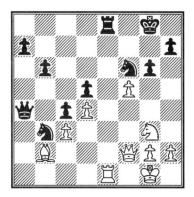

26.Re6! Capablanca seems to have misjudged White's dynamic possibilities. Positionally, the great Cuban is quite OK, but a variety of tactical circumstances, inherent in White's layout of the game, come to Botvinnik's rescue, justifying his abandonment of the queenside. **26...Rxe6.** Or 26...Kf7; 27.Rxf6+ Kxf6; 28.fxg6+ Kxg6; 29.Qf5+ Kg7; 30.Nh5+ Kh6; 31.h4 Rg8; 32.g4 Qc6; 33.Ba3 and White wins.

27.fxe6 Kg7; 28.Qf4 Qe8; 29.Qe5 Qe7.

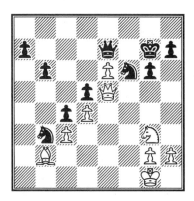

30.Ba3!! A brilliant deflection of the Black queen. **30...Qxa3; 31.Nh5+! gxh5; 32.Qg5+ Kf8; 33.Qxf6+ Kg8; 34.e7.** Of course Botvinnik had to see that there was no perpetual check when he played 30.Ba3. **34...Qc1+; 35.Kf2 Qc2+; 36.Kg3 Qd3+; 37.Kh4 Qe4+; 38.Kxh5 Qe2+; 39.Kh4 Qe4+; 40.g4 Qe1+; 41.Kh5. Black resigned.**

(38) BOTVINNIK - PORTISCH
Monte Carlo, 1968

Portisch was one of the top players of the "early Informant" era, which started with the first publication of the Yugoslavia-based *Chess Informant* in 1966, lasting until about 1980 when computer databases began to appear. He is still a strong player, qualifying for the FIDE World Chapionship Tournament in 1997. He has not had great success against World Champions, however, as we see in this game. **1.c4 e5; 2.Nc3 Nf6; 3.g3 d5; 4.cxd5 Nxd5; 5.Bg2 Be6; 6.Nf3 Nc6; 7.0–0 Nb6.**

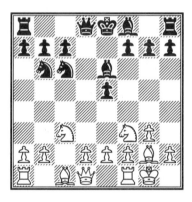

Although Portisch is playing the White side of a Dragon Sicilian minus one tempo, which should be satisfactory for Black, the disadvantage of the White set-up is that its strategic objectives are limited (mainly pressure in the c-file) and it should be possible for Black to parry this while organizing counterplay in the center. **8.d3 Be7; 9.a3 a5; 10.Be3 0–0; 11.Na4 Nxa4.** Botvinnik himself recommended 11...Nd4. **12.Qxa4 Bd5; 13.Rfc1.**

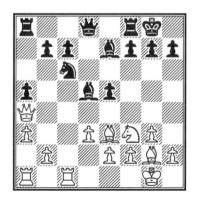

13...Re8. This move betrays a fundamentally incorrect attitude towards the problems of defense. The rook should remain, for the moment, on f8, while Black concentrates on ...f7-f5, followed by ...Bd6 or ...Bf6, taking his share of central command. It seems, however, that Portisch has devised an ingenious scheme to frustrate White's strategic dispositions on the queenside, therefore he is in no hurry to take positive action himself.

14.Rc2 Bf8; 15.Rac1.

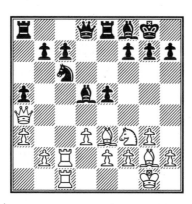

15...Nb8?! Springing his trap, now that White cannot retreat, Black threatens complete consolidation with 16...c6 (after which Botvinnik's pieces would all be marooned on absurd squares) and Portisch doubtless believed that 16.Rxc7 was impossible, since the rook could never escape.

In fact, after 16.Rxc7 Bc6; 17.R7xc6 Nxc6, White has compensation for the exchange and the chances would be balanced. Was this the continuation expected by Portisch? Actually, the best for Black at this point would have been 15...e4; 16.dxe4 Bxe4; 17.Rd2, though White still has the upper hand.

16.Rxc7 Bc6. All according to plan, but there is a terrible shock coming. **17.R1xc6!** It looks insane, since the c7-rook is still trapped, but to quote Botvinnik himself: "In reality this rook has a decisive part to play in the attack. By eliminating Black's light-squared bishop, White gains control of the central light squares."

17...bxc6.

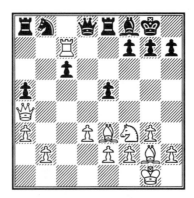

18.Rxf7!! The true point of Botvinnik's combination, and the most majestic orchestration we have ever seen of the ancient theme of the sacrifice against f7. What makes this sacrifice so impressive (apart from the fact that it was completely unexpected) is the brilliant explosion of combinative energy arising from quietly logical strategic play. (Botvinnik uses pressure on the c-file, positional exchange sacrifice, and erosion of Black's light square control.)

Even the direction of the sacrificial blow is original, since such sacrifices against f7 tend to be aimed vertically rather than horizontally. How far we have come from Greco-N.N. or Von der Lasa-Mayet! **18...h6.** or 18...Kxf7; 19.Qc4+ Kg6; 20.Qg4+ Kf7; 21.Ng5+ Kg8; 22.Qc4+ Kh8; 23.Nf7+ and White wins. The point of Black's 18th move is to stop Nf3-g5.

19.Rb7 Qc8; 20.Qc4+ Kh8. If Black seeks relief with 20...Qe6 then 21.Nxe5 gives White an easy win, with three pawns for the exchange.

21.Nh4!! Another brilliant stroke, the final stake in the heart of Black's light squares. **21...Qxb7; 22.Ng6+ Kh7; 23.Be4 Bd6.** To prevent 24.Ne7+ and 25.Qg8 mate, but in any case he cannot avoid a scintillating finale.

24.Nxe5+ g6; 25.Bxg6+ Kg7.

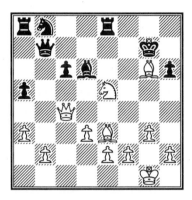

26.Bxh6+!! Black resigned. 26...Kxh6; 27.Qh4+ Kg7; 28.Qh7+ Kf6; 29.Ng4+ Ke6; 30.Qxb7 and White wins. "An extraordinary game for the present time" is how Botvinnik himself descibed it.

(39) BOTVINNIK - TARTAKOWER
Nottingham, 1936

The great international tournament in Nottingham is another of the most famous in chess history. It featured a very strong and varied field. Here we have a clash between the Romantic School, represented by Tartakower, and the new Soviet School in the form of Botvinnik.

1.Nf3 Nf6; 2.c4 d6; 3.d4 Nbd7; 4.g3 e5; 5.Bg2 Be7; 6.0–0 0–0; 7.Nc3 c6; 8.e4 Qc7; 9.h3 Re8; 10.Be3.

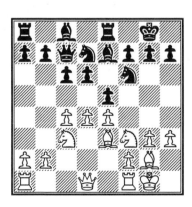

Black's position is constricted. White uses the advantage in space to build an attack. The key idea is to open up a file on the kingside, and the f-file is the logical candidate.

10...Nf8?; 11.Rc1 h6; 12.d5 Bd7; 13.Nd2 g5?; 14.f4 gxf4; 15.gxf4. The g-file is now open, and Black cannot prevent another highway from being constructed on the f-file.

15...Kg7; 16.fxe5 dxe5; 17.c5 cxd5; 18.Nxd5 Qc6; 19.Nc4 Ng6. 19...Bxc5? would be a losing blunder after 20.Rxf6 Bxe3+; 21.Ncxe3 Qb5; 22.Nc7 and **White wins. 20.Nd6 Be6.** 20...Bxd6? loses to 21.Nxf6 Bc7; 22.Qxd7.

21.Nxe7 Nxe7.

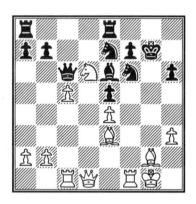

Capturing the rook at e8 is the obvious move, but instead of winning material, Botvinnik decides to sacrifice! In any case, 21...Rxe7; 22.Nf5+ Bxf5; 23.exf5 wins a piece for White. **22.Rxf6!! Kxf6; 23.Qh5.** The threat is 24.Qh6+ Ng6; 25.Bg5#.

23...Ng6; 24.Nf5! Rg8. 24...Bxf5?; 25.exf5! leaves Black powerless against the threats at c6 and g6. 25...e4; 26.fxg6 and White wins. 24...Rh8; 25.h4! leads to another elegant win: 25...Bxa2; 26.Rd1 Rae8.

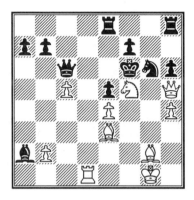

Do you see the combination which leads to mate? **27.Qg5+!!** hxg5; 28.Bxg5+ Ke6; 29.Ng7#. **25.Qxh6.** The bishop eyes the mate at g5. **25...Bxa2; 26.Rd1.** Black faces the deadly threat of Rd6+. **26...Rad8; 27.Qg5+ Ke6; 28.Rxd8 f6.** 28...Rxd8; 29.Qxd8 and Black can resign. **29.Rxg8 Nf4.** 29...fxg5; 30.Rxg6+ Kd7; 31.Rxc6 wins easily. **30.Qg7. Black resigns.**

(40) BOTVINNIK - BATUYEV
Leningrad Championship, 1930

Botvinnik's handling of the isolated d-pawn position was superb, from either side of the board. The player with the isolated pawn usually has an initiative and an advantage in space and maneuverability. Is it any surprise, then, that such positions were very appealing to Botvinnik?

1.d4 d5; 2.c4 e6; 3.Nc3 Nf6; 4.Bg5 Be7; 5.e3 0-0; 6.Nf3 Nbd7; 7.Bd3 dxc4; 8.Bxc4 c5; 9.0-0 cxd4; 10.exd4 Nb6; 11.Bb3 Nbd5; 12.Ne5 Nd7; 13.Bxe7 Nxe7; 14.Qe2 Nf6; 15.Rfd1 b6; 16.Rac1 Bb7.

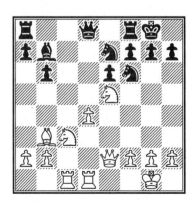

This is a typical isolated d-pawn position in the Queen's Gambit. In return for the weak pawn at d4, White has freedom of movement and control of more space. Although the Black king is protected by a phalanx of pawns, two knights, and a rook, with only the White knight in attacking formation, the weakness of the a2-g8 diagonal is more significant than it seems. **17.f3! Rc8.** Black should have blockaded the diagonal with ...Ned5.

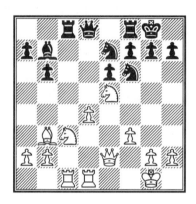

Botvinnik now offers up his only attacking piece to open up the key diagonal. **18.Nxf7! Rxf7; 19.Qxe6 Qf8.** This is the only try. 19...Ned5; 20.Nxd5 Nxd5; 21.Bxd5 Bxd5 allows 22.Rxc8, exploiting the overworked rook.

20.Ne4. The threat is simply Rxc8 followed by Nd6 with a monster fork. **20...Rxc1; 21.Rxc1.** White threatens to trade everything at f7 and then fork with Nd6+.

21...Nfd5; 22.Nd6 Ba8.

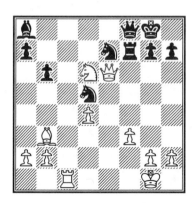

It looks as though Black has weathered the storm. Botvinnik now adds the subtle crowning point to the combination. **23.Re1! g6; 24.Nxf7 Qxf7; 25.Qxe7. Black resigned.**

(41) YURGIS - BOTVINNIK
Leningrad, 1931

When playing against Botvinnik, one would think that it would be a good idea to keep the initiative out of his hands. Challengers such as Vassily Smyslov, Mikhail Tal and Tigran Petrosian understood that, and were able to take the title from him. This game was played before Botvinnik was famous. The game begins as a quiet Réti Opening. Too quiet, for the initiative steadily drifts to Black. The combination lies well into the endgame, rewarding Botvinnik's patience with a polished gem.

1.Nf3 Nf6; 2.c4 c5; 3.Nc3 b6; 4.g3 Bb7; 5.Bg2 d5; 6.cxd5 Nxd5; 7.0–0 e6; 8.b3 Be7; 9.Bb2 0–0.

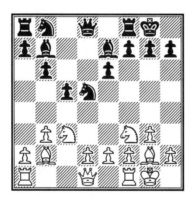

Black has a flexible position, and the king sleeps safely at g8. **10.Nxd5 Bxd5; 11.d3 Nd7; 12.Qc2 Rc8; 13.Rae1 b5; 14.e4 Bb7; 15.Nd2 Nb8!** This knight is only temporarily in retreat. It is headed for d4 via c6.

16.f4 Nc6; 17.a3 Qd7; 18.Nf3 Rfd8; 19.Rd1 Ba6; 20.Ba1. White's passive play has conceded the initiative to Black. **20...b4!; 21.a4 Nd4.** 21...Bxd3?; 22.Qb2 Bf6; 23.e5 Be7; 24.Ne1 would be a disaster for Black.

22.Qb2 Bf6; 23.e5 Be7; 24.Nxd4 cxd4; 25.Qe2 Rc5; 26.Bb2 f5; 27.h4.

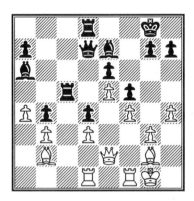

Here Botvinnik uses a sacrifice which is based on long-term investment. The combination comes later. **27...Rc3!; 28.Bxc3 dxc3; 29.Qe3 Bxd3.** 29...Qc7; 30.Rf2 Rd4! would have been stronger, according to Botvinnik, because of the latent threat of Bc5. The a7-g1 diagonal plays a very significant role in this game.

30.Rf2 Qd4; 31.Qxd4 Rxd4; 32.Bf1. 32.Bf3 Bc5; 33.Kg2 c2; 34.Rc1 would have led to the same sort of combination as the game. **32...c2; 33.Rc1.** White cannot capture: 33.Rxc2? Bxc2; 34.Rxd4 Bc5 and the pin wins.

33...Bxf1; 34.Rcxf1.

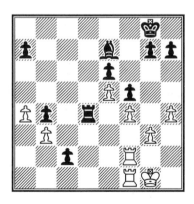

Black would win on either other capture, though not as spectacularly. 34.Kxf1 Rd1+ wins at least a rook. 34.Rfxf1 Rd2 sets up the threat of ...Bc5 after which the bishop can work its way to d2.

35.Rfe1 Bc5+; 36.Kh1 Bd4 and b2 is the next stop. **34...Rc4!!** Black offers up a whole rook, to create the juggernaut of passed pawns on the sixth and seventh rank. The two rooks are no match for the bishop and pair of pawns! **35.bxc4.** 35.Rc1 Bc5; 36.Kf1 Bxf2; 37.Kxf2 Rc3 is a winning endgame for Black.

    35...Bc5; 36.Kg2 Bxf2; 37.Kxf2 b3.

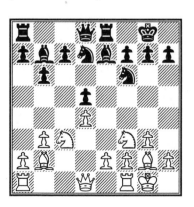

    White resigned. Working together, the two pawns were too much for the rook.

(42) BOTVINNIK - PADEVSKY
Monte Carlo, 1968

Botvinnik was able to turn normally quiet flank games into tactical brawls, usually landing all the punches himself. Here he transforms the center and opens up lines for the kingside attack.

    1.Nf3 Nf6; 2.c4 e6; 3.g3 d5; 4.Bg2 Be7; 5.0–0 0–0; 6.d4 Nbd7; 7.b3 b6; 8.Bb2 Bb7; 9.cxd5 exd5; 10.Nc3 Re8.

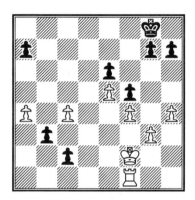

Many players might quietly move a rook here, but Botvinnik wants to control the center so that kingside operations can be activated. **11.Ne5 Bd6; 12.f4 Ne4; 13.Nxe4 dxe4; 14.e3.** The future of the attack is promising, since Black's bishop at b7 and rook at a8 cannot participate in the defense.

14...Nf6; 15.a3 c5. Black tries to gain space on the queenside, but this allows the bishop at b2 to take a larger role in the game. **16.Qe2 cxd4; 17.Bxd4 Qe7; 18.b4!** White needs to keep an eye on the queenside, too.

18...a5; 19.b5 Bxe5; 20.Bxe5.

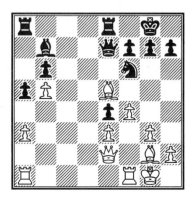

Now the White kingside attack can proceed by advancing the f-pawn to f6. **20...Nd7; 21.Bd4 Nc5; 22.f5 Nd7.** Black could try to stop White's plan with 22...f6, but then 23.Qc4+ Kh8; 24.Bxc5 wins.

23.f6!

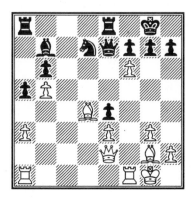

23...Qe6. 23...Nxf6; 24.Rxf6! gxf6; 25.Qg4+ Kf8; 26.Qh4 Qd6; 27.Qxh7 is great for White, because the threat of Rf1 is intense. 23...gxf6; 24.Qg4+ Kh8. (24...Kf8; 25.Qh4 also wins.) 25.Rxf6! is another spectacular win. After 25...Nxf6; 26.Rf1, the game is over.

24.Qh5 Ne5. 24...gxf6; 25.Bh3 Qd6; 26.Bxd7 Qxd7; 27.Bxf6 and Black can resign. 24...Nxf6; 25.Rxf6 is given by Botvinnik without further comment, but the win is not easy. 25...gxf6; 26.Bh3 Qd6; 27.Bf5 Kf8; 28.Qxh7 Bd5; 29.Rf1. White can now target either the pawn at f6 with Qh4, or the one at e4, via Rf4. **25.Rf5 Ng6.** 25...g6 lets the queen infiltrate at h6. 25...Nf3+; 26.Bxf3 exf3; 27.Qg5 also wins. **26.fxg7.**

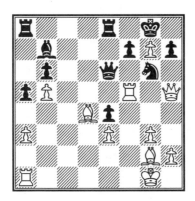

White has a cute threat, which his opponent allows to be displayed. **26...Rad8.** 26...Ne7; 27.Rf6 Qd5; 28.Qg4. White will finally harvest the pawn at b6, or can continue to go after f7, with an overwhelming advantage in either case. **27.Qxh7+. Black resigned,** as 27...Kxh7; 28.Rh5+ Kg8; 29.Rh8+ Nxh8; 30.gxh8Q# is checkmate.

FIND THE WIN!

(25) BOTVINNIK - KERES
World Championship, The Hague, 1948

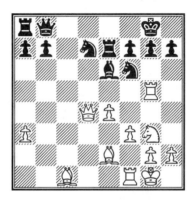

The king is well defended and there is only a rook attacking. How do you continue the onslaught and bring quick victory for White?

(26) STOLBERG - BOTVINNIK
Soviet Championship, 1940

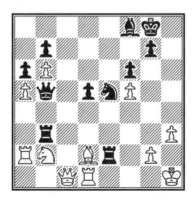

Black's forces are concentrated on the queenside and on the seventh rank, but the winning blow takes place far away. Open the necessary lines to finish the game with a flourish!

(27) GOGLIDZE - BOTVINNIK
Moscow, 1935

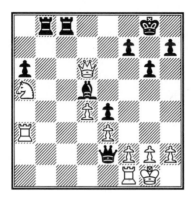

There's nobody at home! Time to invade!

(28) LILIENTHAL - BOTVINNIK
Moscow, 1941

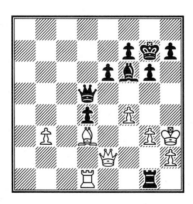

Black can force the win of a second pawn, which is enough to bring about a decisive advantage. How is this accomplished?

10. VASSILY SMYSLOV

Seventh World Champion (1957–1958)

Smyslov presents quite a contrast to his predecessor. Instead of striving impatiently for the initiative, Smyslov became the master of the art of maneuvering. He strove to coordinate his pieces at all times, in the opening, the middlegame, and the endgame. Many opening variations bear his name, in the Spanish Game, Grünfeld Defense, King's Indian Defense, Slav Defense and many other openings.

The endgame was of particular interest to Smyslov. He is the co-author of a famous treatise on rook and pawn endgames. His recent book, *Endgame Virtuoso*, is well deserving of its title. Still, he was able to spot brilliant combinations when opportunities arose.

In a Smyslovian combination, the groundwork is laid by thorough preparation. Pieces are stealthily maneuvered into position, often seeming to be aimed at some irrelevant goal. Sometimes, the position explodes into a fierce, but brief, battle before the opponent lays down his arms. In other cases, a combination leads to a winning endgame. Smyslov's sacrifices are based on an evaluation of the positional value of the pieces, and the results of his combinations must take into account the positional value of the pieces as well as their nominal values.

(43) SMYSLOV - GEREBEN
Moscow - Budapest, 1949

Being fond of coordination does not mean that gambit play is out of the question. On the contrary, in gambits the excellent coordination of pieces contributes heavily to the compensation for the sacrificed material. The opening of this game is known as the Fantasy Variation, and, especially when it leads to a gambit, as here, has led to some fantastic games!

1.e4 c6; 2.d4 d5; 3.f3. The fantasy begins with this move. **3...e6; 4.Be3 dxe4; 5.Nd2 exf3; 6.Ngxf3 Nf6; 7.Nc4 Nd5; 8.Bd2 Be7; 9.Bd3.**

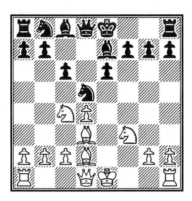

Black has accepted the gambit, which means that accurate defense is required. **9...Bh4+?** A critical mistake. The check achieves nothing more than a loss of time. 9...Bf6 is the most logical move, and Black has a solid position. Still, White has sufficient compensation for the pawn.

10.g3 Bf6; 11.Qe2 a5; 12.a3 0–0.

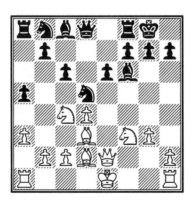

13.h4! Be7. 13...Nd7 falls for the classic combination 14.Bxh7+!! Kxh7; 15.Ng5+ Bxg5; 16.hxg5+ Kg8; 17.Qh5 and **White wins.** **14.Ng5** Now the sacrifice would fail: 14.Bxh7+ Kxh7; 15.Ng5+ Kg8; 16.Qh5 Nf6 and Black defends. **14...Nf6; 15.Ne5 b5.** 15...Qxd4 gives White a strong attack after 16.Bc3! Qc5; 17.Rf1 h6 where the sacrifice of the rook at f6 works just as well as in the game. 18.Rxf6!!

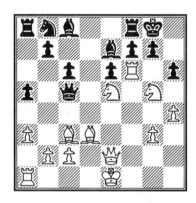

White is in charge, as the following variations show: 18...Bxf6; 19.Ne4. (19.Qe4 g6; 20.Bd4 Qd6; 21.Nexf7 Rxf7; 22.Qxg6+ Rg7; 23.Qxf6 is a win for White. 18...Kg7 loses spectacularly to 19.Qxh6+!! The capture with the pawn is no better: 18...gxf6; 19.Ne4 Qg1+; 20.Kd2 Qxa1; 21.Qg4+ Kh8; 22.Nxf6 Bxf6; 23.Qe4 and Black cannot avoid mate!)

But that is not how the game went. Instead Black has advanced the b-pawn, and then the tension rose with

16.Rf1 h6.

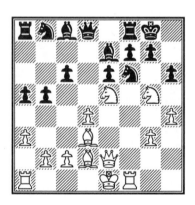

17.Rxf6! Black avoided this earlier, but now it is inevitable. The combination forces the win. **17...gxf6.** 17...Bxf6; 18.Bh7+ Kh8; 19.Nexf7+ Rxf7; 20.Nxf7+ Kxh7; 21.Qd3+ Kg8; 22.Nxd8 Bxd8; 23.Qg6 is a winning position for White.

18.Qh5 fxg5; 19.Qxh6.

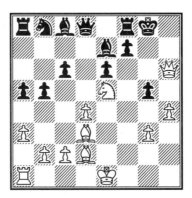

The winning procedure is simply a matter of opening the h-file. Black's pieces are in no position to defend the king. **19...f5; 20.Qg6+ Kh8; 21.hxg5 Bxa3; 22.Ke2 Qd5; 23.Nf3 1–0.**

(44) BOTVINNIK - SMYSLOV
World Championship , 1954

Although Botvinnik won this first World Championship match, Smyslov got a few good shots in. This game involves both a positional sacrifice and a nice combination, an example of Smyslov at his best.

1.d4 Nf6; 2.c4 g6; 3.g3 Bg7; 4.Bg2 0–0; 5.Nc3 d6; 6.Nf3 Nbd7; 7.0–0 e5; 8.e4 c6; 9.Be3 Ng4; 10.Bg5 Qb6; 11.h3 exd4!; 12.Na4 Qa6; 13.hxg4 b5; 14.Nxd4 bxa4; 15.Nxc6 Qxc6.

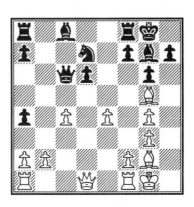

White now uses a simple tactic to win the exchange, but Smyslov had taken this into account. This is not a combination, because White could have chosen other plans instead. **16.e5 Qxc4; 17.Bxa8 Nxe5.** Black has more than enough compensation. Just look at the pawn at g4, the passed d-pawn and the general weakness of the light squares. **18.Rc1 Qb4; 19.a3 Qxb2; 20.Qxa4 Bb7; 21.Rb1.** 21.Bxb7 Qxb7; 22.Rc3 h6; 23.Bf4 Nf3+; 24.Rxf3 Qxf3; 25.Bxd6 Rd8; 26.Bc5 would have been roughly level, according to Smyslov.

21...Nf3+! The combined force of the knight and bishop at b7 give a high potency to this attack.

22.Kh1.

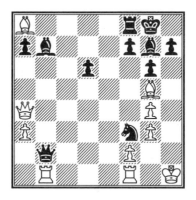

22...Bxa8! Smyslov parts with the queen, but gets a winning position as a result. This is a combination, in the sense that White's reply is forced.

23.Rxb2 Nxg5+; 24.Kh2 Nf3+; 25.Kh3 Bxb2; 26.Qxa7 Be4.

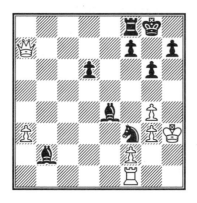

Black's three minor pieces are more than a match for the king. **27.a4 Kg7; 28.Rd1 Be5; 29.Qe7 Rc8; 30.a5 Rc2.** White is attacking with just a lone queen, but all four of Black's pieces are participating. **31.Kg2 Nd4+; 32.Kf1 Bf3; 33.Rb1 Nc6. White resigned.** Black's pieces are beautifully coordinated and the primary threat is ...Bd4.

(45) SMYSLOV - BOTVINNIK
World Championship, Moscow, 1954

It is very rare that a player will leave the king in the center in a World Championship match! This is a dangerous strategy, especially for Black. Although the strong pawn structure in the center in the French Defense would seem to afford sufficient protection, Smyslov shows that not to be the case.

1.e4 e6; 2.d4 d5; 3.Nc3 Bb4; 4.e5 c5; 5.a3 Ba5. Normally Black captures at c3, but this retreat leads to complications with a very unbalanced pawn structure.

6.b4 cxd4; 7.Qg4 Ne7; 8.bxa5 dxc3.

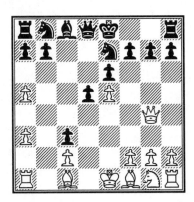

White's queenside pawns are very weak, and the pawn at c3 is an annoyance, but White will pick up g7 and h7 and have an outside passed pawn. **9.Qxg7 Rg8; 10.Qxh7 Nd7?!** This knight belongs on c6. Now White will execute a very simple plan — advance the h-pawn until it becomes a queen! Of course he will have to be careful in the execution of the strategy.

11.Nf3 Nf8. Botvinnik proposed 11...Qc7 as an improvement, but Smyslov correctly points out that White has a strong reply: 11...Qc7; 12.Bb5! For example: 12...Rxg2?!; 13.Kf1 Rg8; 14.Rg1 Rxg1+; 15.Kxg1 and the pin makes it very hard for Black to develop.

12.Qd3 Qxa5; 13.h4. Here we go! It turns out that Black's pawn at c3 just gets in the way. **13...Bd7; 14.Bg5!** Black is prevented from castling, and the control of the h4-d8 diagonal keeps Black pinned down. Smyslov deftly exploits this fact and his h-pawn. **14...Rc8; 15.Nd4!** Black was going to try and wiggle out using Rc8-c4-e4+ and the placement of a knight at f5. This stops both plans.

15...Nf5.

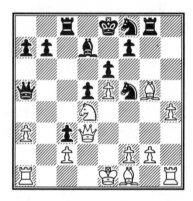

Now White does not want to capture immediately, because the Nf8 would occupy the new hole at e6. But how to answer the threat of Nf5xd4 and Bb5? **16.Rb1! Rc4?!** Smyslov considers 16...b6 best, but it is hard to blame Botvinnik, for what follows is truly inspired.

17.Nxf5 exf5; 18.Rxb7 Re4+.

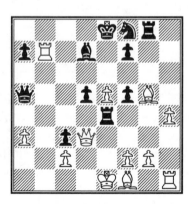

The weakness of the back rank is fatal. The combination is based on the correct evaluation of the endgame. **19.Qxe4!! dxe4; 20.Rb8+ Bc8; 21.Bb5+ Qxb5.** 21...Nd7; 22.Rxc8+.

22.Rxb5.

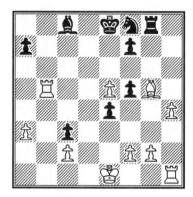

Smyslov appreciated that the h-pawn is a juggernaut which cannot be stopped. **22...Ne6; 23.Bf6 Rxg2; 24.h5 Ba6; 25.h6!** It is only fitting that the pawn has the final say. After the bishop captures the rook there is no way to stop the pawn from queening. **Black resigned.**

(46) GELLER - SMYSLOV
Moscow USSR, 1965

World Champions sometimes find themselves on the wrong end of a brilliant combination, as we have already seen. Here Yefim Geller, often a candidate for the World Championship himself, hands out a lesson in combinative technique.

1.d4 Nf6; 2.c4 g6; 3.Nc3 d5; 4.cxd5 Nxd5; 5.e4 Nxc3; 6.bxc3 Bg7; 7.Bc4 c5; 8.Ne2 0–0; 9.0–0 Nc6; 10.Be3 Qc7. Smyslov's own variation which plans to bombard White's pawn-center with pressure from the Black pieces, especially the g7-bishop. **11.Rc1 Rd8; 12.f4 e6; 13.Kh1 b6?** An inaccuracy which costs Smyslov dearly. Correct is 13...Na5!; 14.Bd3 f5 restraining White's kingside expansion.

14.f5 Na5; 15.Bd3 exf5; 16.exf5 Bb7; 17.Qd2 Re8; 18.Ng3 Qc6; 19.Rf2 Rad8. Inadequate is the "thematic combination" 19...Rxe3; 20.Qxe3 cxd4; 21.cxd4 Bxd4; 22.Qf4! Qxc1+; 23.Qxc1 Bxf2; 24.Qh6 and **White wins**.

20.Bh6.

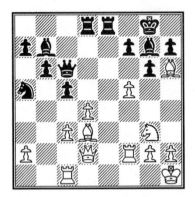

20...Bh8. The beginning of a sad career for Black's ambitious h8-bishop. The dark squares around his king (f6/h6) are looking ominously exposed. **21.Qf4 Rd7; 22.Ne4 c4.** Not 22...Rxe4; 23.Bxe4 Qxe4; 24.Qb8+. **23.Bc2 Rde7; 24.Rcf1! Rxe4.** Falling in with Geller's intentions, which comprise a combination of rare beauty. Without this capture, however, Black would have no defense against White's threat to open the flood gates of the f-file.

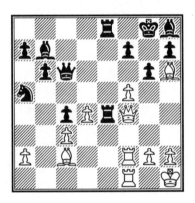

25.fxg6!! f6. If 25...Rxf4; 26.gxh7# or 25...Qxg6; 26.Qxf7+ Qxf7; 27.Rxf7 Re1 to prevent mate on f8, 28.Bxh7#. **26.Qg5! Qd7.** Once again mate on f8 looms if Black captures the queen.

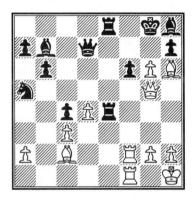

27.Kg1!! A very deep move, Black is placed in a kind of sus-pended animation, but that is not the sole point, as we shall see.

27...Bg7; 28.Rxf6 Rg4.

The alternative 28...Bxf6 reveals the profundity of Geller's 27th move: 29.Qxf6 hxg6; 30.Qxg6+ Kh8; 31.Bg5 R4e6; 32.Bf6+ Rxf6; 33.Rxf6 and Black is defenseless, precisely because he can derive no profit from 33...Re1+.

29.gxh7+ Kh8; 30.Bxg7+ Qxg7; 31.Qxg4! 31...Qxg4; 32.Rf8+ finito. Geller sacrificed his queen no less than four times, yet she survived to see Black's resignation. **1–0.**

(47) SMYSLOV - LIBERZON
Moscow, 1969

Smyslov understood the fianchetto position well. When he used it, he was rarely willing to surrender his fianchettoed bishop, and would sometimes even sacrifice material to preserve it. In this game, his opponent undervalues the piece and lets it leave the board. The weakness of the dark squares enables the powerful combination which leads to a win for Smyslov.

1.c4 g6; 2.Nc3 Bg7; 3.d4 Nf6; 4.Bg5 c5; 5.e3 cxd4; 6.exd4 d5.

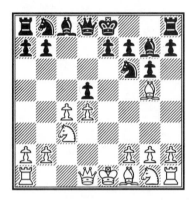

The game has transposed from the English Opening to the Panov Attack. The same position could have arisen on 1.e4 c6; 2.d4 d5; 3.exd5 cxd5; 4.c4 Nf6; 5.Nc3 g6; 6.Bg5 Bg7. White can win a pawn here, and indeed the simple 7.cxd5 is more often met by castling and regaining the pawn later, rather than the immediate capture with the knight.

7.Bxf6 Bxf6; 8.cxd5 0–0; 9.Nf3 Nd7; 10.Bc4 Nb6; 11.Bb3 Bg4; 12.0–0 Rc8; 13.Re1.

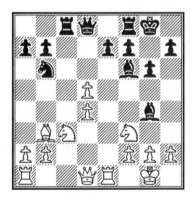

Black now decides to regain the pawn and work on the c-file. To do so, he must part with his pride and joy, the dark squared bishop. That is too high a price! **13...Bxf3; 14.Qxf3 Bxd4; 15.Rad1 Bxc3; 16.bxc3 Qd6; 17.h4.** Naturally White decides to attack the weakened kingside. **17...h5; 18.Rd4 Kg7; 19.Rf4 Rc7; 20.Re6 Qd8; 21.Re3 Qd6.** Black is defending well, and White must find another strategy.

22.Rfe4 a5; 23.a4 Qf6; 24.Rf4 Qd6.

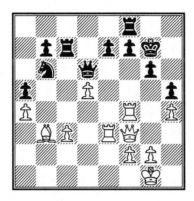

Black's pawns seem to offer sufficient defense for the king, and the White bishop plays no part. Yet there is a combination here, and Smyslov spots it. **25.Re6!! Qc5.** 25...fxe6; 26.Rxf8 is out of the question. **26.Rxg6+!!** The rook will not be denied its sacrificial role. Now the f-file is open at last. **26...fxg6.** 26...Kxg6; 27.Bc2+ f5; 28.Rxf5 and mate follows.

27.Rxf8 Qxc3.

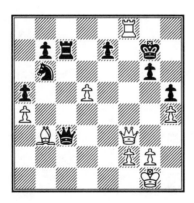

Black has an extra pawn, but that is hardly relevant. The Black king cannot survive for long. **28.Qf7+ Kh6; 29.Qf4+ Kg7; 30.Rf7+ Kg8; 31.d6! Qxb3; 32.Rf8+. Black resigned.**

(48) UHLMANN - SMYSLOV
Moscow, 1971
1.c4 Nf6; 2.Nc3 e6; 3.Nf3 b6; 4.g3 Bb7; 5.Bg2 Be7; 6.0-0 0-0; 7.d4 Ne4; 8.Bd2 d5; 9.cxd5 exd5.

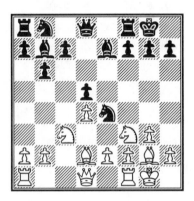

The result of the opening is a quiet variation of the Queen's Indian Defense. Black has a comfortable game, and can quickly go to work on the center by advancing the c-pawn to c5. Black will obtain a queenside pawn majority which can be useful in the endgame.

10.Rc1 Nd7; 11.Bf4 c5; 12.dxc5 Nxc3; 13.bxc3 Nxc5; 14.Be5 Re8; 15.Re1 Ne4; 16.Qa4 a6; 17.c4 Bc5; 18.e3 dxc4; 19.Qxc4 Rc8; 20.Qe2. Black has achieved beautiful coordination of his pieces, and White's seem to lack purpose. It is clear that the Black army is more deserving of the initiative. There are obstacles to be overcome, however.

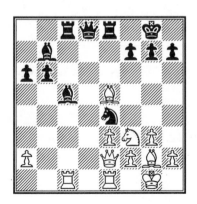

White's king is well-defended. Black must somehow try to crack through the barrier. A combination fires up the attack and scorches enemy territory. **20...Nxf2!!; 21.Qxf2 Bxf3.** Now if White recaptures at f3, the bishop at e5 falls. So instead, White counterattacks the enemy rook at c8.

22.Bh3 Rxe5; 23.Bxc8 Bc6.

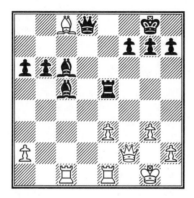

White has an extra exchange for a pawn, but nothing to attack. Black's bishops rake the kingside from a safe distance, and are, therefore, very dangerous. **24.Bh3.** 24.Bxa6 would lose instantly to 24...Qd5! **24...Qe8; 25.Bg2.**

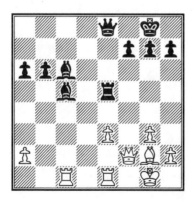

White tries to exchange bishops, eliminating threats on the light squares. Smyslov has eyes for the dark squares, however. **25...Rxe3!; 26.Kh1.** 26.Bxc6 Rxe1+; 27.Rxe1 Qxe1+ wins everything. **26...Bxg2+; 27.Kxg2 Qe4+.** Smyslov returns to the light squares to clean up. **28.Kh3 Qe6+; 29.Kg2 Qd5+; 30.Kh3 Re6. White resigned.**

FIND THE WIN!

(29) SMYSLOV - HÜBNER
Candidates' Match, 1983

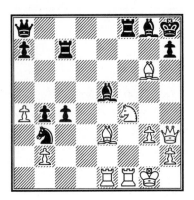

This one isn't easy. It takes many moves to finish Black off, but Smyslov found the key moves and so can you!

(30) SMYSLOV - DONNER
Havana, 1966

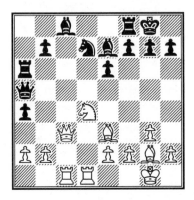

White would love to play Nc6, forking a5 and e7, but that isn't possible, yet.

(31) SMYSLOV - FLOHR
Soviet Championship, 1949

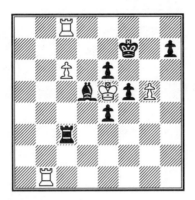

Mating combinations in the endgame? Why not!

(32) SMYSLOV - KOTTNAUER
Moscow, 1948

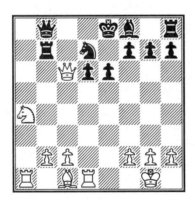

White can exploit Black's unwise reluctance to get castled. How?

11. MIKHAIL TAL

Eighth World Champion (1960–1961)

"The Magician," Mikhail Tal, was the most popular of World Champions. His attacking style and combinational genius was on display throughout his career. He had a passion for attack, and loved to have his creative faculties tested in battle. He delighted in finding a long forcing variation, even in a post-mortem analysis session.

He described the making of combinations as a process which starts with a careful study of the position. This provides the necessary associations on which concrete calculations can be made. Before calculating, however, the master assembles some target positions, without worrying about whether or not they can be reached. These target positions are triggered during the calculating process. Calculation of forced variations leads to one of the target positions, and the goal is achieved.

One could easily fill an entire book with Tal's combinations. Hundreds can be found in the massive four-volume collection of his games published by Chess Stars, though any book containing Tal's games is a sheer delight, since the moves speak for themselves. We have selected a few of our favorites, which are typical of his style.

(49) TAL - ZEID
Riga Soviet Latvia, 1952

Even as a young man, Tal had a flair for combinations, Tal sacrifices a pawn in the opening, which eventually allows him to create a weakness in the enemy position.

1.d4 c6; 2.c4 d5; 3.Nf3 Nf6; 4.Nc3 dxc4; 5.e4!? The usual move is 5.a4, but the gambit offered by Tal can grant formidable attacking chances. **5...b5; 6.e5 Nd5; 7.a4 Nxc3?** Inaccurate. It is better to precede this capture with 7...e6; 8.axb5 Nxc3; 9.bxc3 cxb5 and

Black's c8-bishop enjoys untroubled freedom of action. As played, that bishop becomes little more than a spectator. **8.bxc3 a6; 9.Be2.** Immediate aggression with 9.Ng5 also deserved consideration.

9...Bb7; 10.Ng5 h6; 11.Ne4 e6; 12.Ba3.

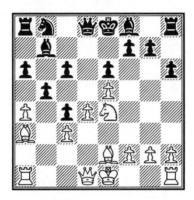

A logical weakening of the opponent's dark squares in order to enhance the power of White's centralized Knight. **12...Bxa3; 13.Rxa3 0–0; 14.0–0 Nd7; 15.f4 Qe7; 16.Ra1 Nb6?** This irrelevant pawn hunt reminds me of one of the early nineteenth-century "defensive" methods. Black had to challenge White's concentration of force on the kingside by means of 16...f5! White would still have a great game after 17.Nd6, but could offer some resistance.16...c5 on the other hand, would be useless after 17.Nd6 Bd5; 18.f5.

17.Qd2 Nxa4; 18.f5 exf5.

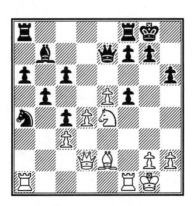

19.Nf6+! The idea of this type of sacrifice is that its acceptance creates a column of useless Black pawns on the f-file, causing a traffic-jam for any pieces that seek to defend the king.

19...Kh8. Or 19...gxf6; 20.Qxh6 fxe5; 21.Rf3 f4; 22.Rh3 f6; 23.Qh8+ Kf7; 24.Rh7+ and **White wins. 20.Rxf5 Rfd8; 21.Raf1 Bc8; 22.Rh5.** Another sacrifice is coming, this time on h6.

22...Qf8; 23.Rf4 Nxc3; 24.Rfh4 Nxe2+.

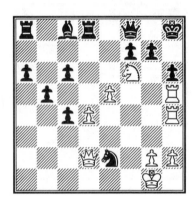

25.Kf2. A bit of humor on the chess-board. The king strolls out into the open, counting on the rook to capture the pawn at h6 quickly and end the game. Black has an extra piece and three pawns, but there is no defense. **25...g5; 26.Rxh6+ Qxh6; 27.Rxh6+ Kg7; 28.Qxg5+ Kf8; 29.Rh8+. Black resigned.**

(50) GURGENIDZE - TAL
Moscow, 1957

The Benoni was one of Tal's favorite openings. It was one of the most popular and aggressive defensive systems against the d-pawn openings in modern tournament practice, though it is now considered a bit suspect. A close relative is the sophisticated Benko (counter) Gambit, 3...b5!?, which also seeks to gain the initiative for Black, rather than merely equalize. This game shows a typical Benoni strategy for Black, one which is aimed at creating the circumstances for a vicious combination.

1.d4 Nf6; 2.c4 c5; 3.d5 e6; 4.Nc3 exd5; 5.cxd5 d6; 6.Nf3 g6; 7.e4 Bg7; 8.Be2 0–0; 9.0–0 Re8; 10.Nd2 Na6.

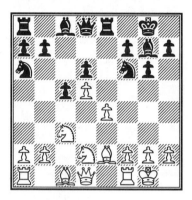

11.Re1. A move which looks natural enough, but involves a barely perceptible weakening of f2. This game was played in the early days of the Modern Benoni and 11.f3! is now accepted as the main line.

11...Nc7; 12.a4 b6; 13.Qc2 Ng4; 14.h3? A superficial reply which permits Tal to bring off a time-honored sacrifice in an entirely modern setting. Correct is 14.Bxg4 Bxg4; 15.Nc4.

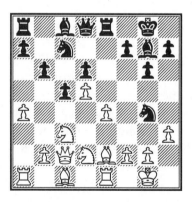

Tal here would conclude from his examination of the position that the primary weakness in White's position is f2. If that pawn falls, then the bishop can seize the critical d4-g1 diagonal from d4, and the Black queen moves into position at h4. Then there will be the additional possibility of a sacrifice at h3. One might assume that the sacrificial lamb would be the cleric at c8, but the pattern has a surprising twist.

14...Nxf2!; 15.Kxf2 Qh4+; 16.Kf1 Bd4; 17.Nd1.

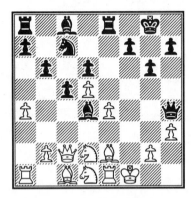

17...Qxh3! The move Gurgenidze had not seen. 18.gxh3 Bxh3 is mate, and, with Black's queen on h3, White's defenses have been completely shattered. **18.Bf3 Qh2; 19.Ne3 f5; 20.Ndc4 fxe4; 21.Bxe4 Ba6; 22.Bf3 Re5; 23.Ra3 Rae8; 24.Bd2 Nxd5.** A fresh acquisition. White evidently cannot capture twice on d5 and his position now collapses. **25.Bxd5+ Rxd5; 26.Ke2 Bxe3; 27.Rxe3 Bxc4+. White resigned.**

(51) TAL - POLUGAYEVSKY,
Tbilisi, 1959

Tal may not have invented the sacrifice at e6 in the Sicilian Defense, but he certainly was one of its leading exponents. The demolition of the center is a prelude to a mopping up of the weakened defenders, and then a simple assault on the enemy king. Here the pursuit continues even into the endgame.

1.e4 c5; 2.Nf3 d6; 3.d4 cxd4; 4.Nxd4 Nf6; 5.Nc3 a6; 6.Bg5 Nbd7; 7.Bc4 Qa5! An improvement on Keres-Sajtar, Amsterdam Olympiad, 1954 where 7...e6?! was played. **8.Qd2 e6; 9.0-0 Be7; 10.Rad1 Nc5?!** Stronger is 10...h6 intending ...g5, trying to dominate the central dark squares.

11.Rfe1 Bd7; 12.a3 Qc7; 13.b4 Na4; 14.Nxa4 Bxa4.

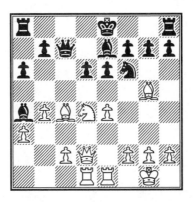

Now we see a very typical tactical maneuver in the Sicilian Defense. **15.Bxe6! fxe6; 16.Nxe6 Qxc2; 17.Qd4 Kf7; 18.Rc1 Qa2.** Black could also surrender the queen (which is often the outcome for the defender against a sacrificial combination) but to no avail: 18...Kxe6; 19.Rxc2 Bxc2; 20.Qc4+ with a win for White. Or 18...Qxc1; 19.Rxc1 Kxe6; 20.Rc7 and **White wins**.

19.e5!? White has a second method of sacrificing his knight: 19.Nxg7 Kxg7; 20.Bxf6+ Bxf6; 21.Rc7+ Kg6; 22.Qxd6, which grants him an even more vehement attack than the text. **19...dxe5.** A better defense is 19...Qxe6; 20.exf6 Bxf6; 21.Bxf6 Rhc8! though Black is still much worse after 22.Bxg7 Rxc1; 23.Rxc1.

20.Qxe5.

20...Qxf2+. Black uses a little combination to go into an endgame, but it is vastly favorable to White since Black's king can find no shelter. **21.Kxf2 Ng4+; 22.Kg1 Nxe5; 23.Rxe5 Bxg5; 24.Nxg5+ Kg6; 25.Ne6 Rhe8; 26.Re3 Rac8; 27.Rf1 Bb5; 28.Rg3+ Kh6; 29.Nxg7.** White has a pawn, and the better attacking chances.

29...Rf8. 29...Bxf1; 30.Nxe8 Rc1 looks strong, but, after the simple 31.Nd6 there is no useful discovered check. **30.Re1 Rf6; 31.h3 Rc2?** 31...Bd7; 32.Kh2 Rc2; 33.Re5 Rg6; 34.Nf5+ Bxf5; 35.Rxf5 is not won yet, but Black is in bad shape in either single rook or double rook endgames. **32.Re4 Rc4; 33.Re5 Rc1+; 34.Kh2. Black resigned.**

(52) POLUGAYEVSKY - TAL
Moscow, 1969

Very few players could out-calculate Tal, who launched more combinations than he fell for, but here is an exception. Tal was not generally known as an opening theorétician, but he did have an intense interest in sharp lines where there were abundant opportunities for combinations.

In this game, the great opening expert Lev Polugayevsky took advantage of this to gain revenge, perhaps, from his defeat a decade earlier which we saw in the previous game. Tal's 13th move was planned as an improvement on Petrosian's handling of the position, but it seems that Polugayevsky was fully prepared to meet it. In fact, we cannot suppress the suspicion that Polugayevsky had worked out his entire combination in pre-game analysis.

1.c4 Nf6; 2.Nc3 e6; 3.Nf3 d5; 4.d4 c5; 5.cxd5 Nxd5; 6.e4 Nxc3; 7.bxc3 cxd4; 8.cxd4 Bb4+.

A simplification is useful to Black. Black should be able to surmount the tactical difficulties caused by White's central predominance and kingside threats and that his queenside pawn majority should then offer him good chances for the ending. In practice, however, Black often falls victim to a sudden raid.

9.Bd2 Bxd2+; 10.Qxd2 0-0; 11.Bc4 Nc6; 12.0-0 b6; 13.Rad1 Na5. This variation had become popular as a result of the interesting 5th match game between Spassky and Petrosian played earlier in 1969, which continued: 13...Bb7; 14.Rfe1 Rc8; 15.d5 exd5; 16.Bxd5 Na5; 17.Qf4! White had a much better game.

14.Bd3 Bb7; 15.Rfe1 Rc8; 16.d5.

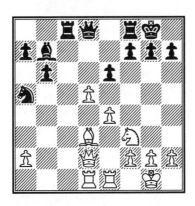

16...exd5. An inspired defensive idea here is the queen "sacrifice" suggested by Matsukevich: 16...Qd6; 17.e5 Qxd5; 18.Qf4 h6; 19.Bh7+ Kxh7; 20.Rxd5 Bxd5 when Black has a very solid position, and has also effected an important simplification.

17.e5! Black's kingside now suffers from a fearful cramp. **17...Nc4.** This turns out to be inferior, but 17...Qe7; 18.Nd4 with a better game for White.

18.Qf4 Nb2. Losing by force, but if 18...h6; 19.Qf5 g6; 20.Qg4 (threatening Bxg6) followed by e5-e6. **19.Bxh7+!** An old-fashioned sacrifice in a modern setting. Against the best defense White cannot force mate, but simply reaches a (materially) level ending. **19...Kxh7; 20.Ng5+ Kg6.** Not 20...Kg8; 21.Qh4 Re8; 22.e6 and **White wins.**

21.h4!

21...Rc4! An excellent defense which avoids two spectacular conclusions: 21...Nxd1; 22.h5+ Kxh5; 23.g4+ Kh6; 24.Qh2+ Kxg5; 25.Qh5+ Kf4; 26.Qf5#. 21...Rh8; 22.Qxf7+ Kh6; 23.Qe6+ Kh5; 24.g4+ Kxh4; 25.Nf3+ Kh3; 26.g5#. Note that Black defends actively, not by seizing even more material. **22.h5+ Kh6; 23.Nxf7+ Kh7; 24.Qf5+ Kg8; 25.e6,** with the terrible threat of 26.h6, but Tal still continues to find ways out.

25...Qf6!

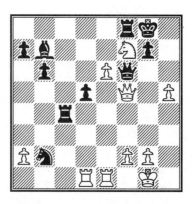

26.Qxf6 gxf6; 27.Rd2. Attacking the knight and also intending Nd6, so White regains his piece. **27...Rc6; 28.Rxb2 Re8; 29.Nh6+ Kh7; 30.Nf5 Rcxe6 31.Rxe6 Rxe6; 32.Rc2 Rc6; 33.Re2.**

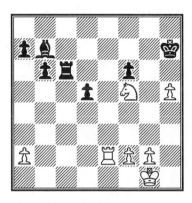

The final result of the combination seems to be only an "equal" ending, but the poor position of Black's king combined with White's active rook leave Tal at a pronounced disadvantage. **33...Bc8?** The only chance to defend was 33...Rc7! protecting the vulnerable second rank. **34.Re7+ Kh8; 35.Nh4** Threatening 36.Ng6+ Kg8; 37.h6 and **White wins**. **35...f5; 36.Ng6+ Kg8; 37.Rxa7 1–0.**

(53) THORBERGSSON - TAL
Reykjavik, 1964
1.d4 Nf6; 2.c4 g6; 3.Nc3 Bg7; 4.e4 0-0; 5.f4 d6; 6.Nf3 c5; 7.d5 e6; 8.Be2 exd5; 9.exd5 b5!?

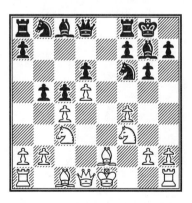

The Benko Gambit idea, mentioned in game 53, surfaces here. After 10.cxb5 a6, Black will obtain good compensation against White's queenside by combining pressure in the open "a" and "b" files with the activity of his g7-bishop. The move f2-f4 is not helpful to white in such situations. **10.Nxb5 Ne4; 11.0–0 a6; 12.Na3?!** Feeble. White should return the pawn with 12.Nc3! Nxc3; 13.bxc3 Bxc3; 14.Rb1. **12...Ra7; 13.Bd3 Re7; 14.Nc2 Rfe8; 15.Re1 Nd7; 16.Ne3 Ndf6; 17.Qc2 Nh5; 18.g3 Bd4!** An original idea. Black is prepared to exchange his bishop in order to increase his control of e3.

19.Nxd4 cxd4; 20.Ng2.

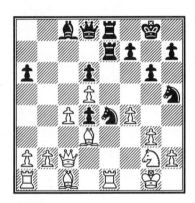

20...Ng5! "Une petite combinaison." **21.Rxe7 Nh3+; 22.Kf1 Rxe7!** Most players would have recaptured with the queen, but see Tal's 25th.

23.Bd2 Nf6; 24.Nh4 Ng4; 25.Nf3 Re3!

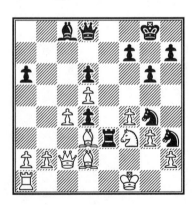

The fireworks are just beginning! **26.Kg2.** The rook is taboo because on Bxe3, Black replies...Nxe3+, winning the enemy queen. 26.Nxd4 leads to a spectacular line. 26...Nxf4; 27.gxf4 Qh4; 28.Be1 Nxh2+; 29.Kg1 Qxf4; 30.Qxh2 Qxd4; 31.Bf2 Qg4+; 32.Qg2 Rxd3; 33.Qxg4 Bxg4 and the three connected, passed pawns will prove too much for White. **26...Qe7; 27.Re1.** Now we see a variation on a theme seen in the previous note. **27...Nxf4+!; 28.gxf4 Rxe1; 29.Nxe1 Qh4; 30.Bc1.** He has to defend f2. **30...Qxe1; 31.h3 Nh6.** Black is winning now. **32.f5 Nxf5; 33.Bf4 Nh4+; 34.Kh2 Nf3+; 35.Kg2 Bxh3+! 36.Kxf3 Qg1.** 37.Bxg6 Qg4+; 38.Kf2 Qxf4+; 39.Kg1 hxg6. **White resigned.**

(54) BOTTERILL - TAL
European Team Championship, 1973

Tal won the brilliancy prize for the following game, but the winning combination came about as a result of adjournment analysis by Tal and the Soviet team, although this fact does not exclude the possibility that he would have seen the combination even without adjourning. The first part of the game is unremarkable, but is worth playing through to see how the critical position came about.

1.e4 c5; 2.Nf3 e6; 3.Nc3 a6; 4.d4 cxd4; 5.Nxd4 Qc7; 6.Bd3 Nf6; 7.0-0 Nc6; 8.Nb3 b5; 9.Bg5 Be7; 10.Qe2 Bb7; 11.Rae1 d6; 12.a3 b4; 13.axb4 Nxb4; 14.Ra1 0-0; 15.Na5 Bc8; 16.Bc4 Rb8; 17.f4 d5; 18.e5 Bc5+; 19.Kh1 Nd7; 20.Bd3 Nxd3; 21.Qxd3 Rxb2; 22.Nb3 Bb4; 23.Na2.

23...Nc5?! 23...Ba3! was stronger, and would have equalized.
24.Qd4 Ba3; 25.Qc3 Qb6; 26.Nd2 Rxa2; 27.Rxa2 Bb4; 28.Qb2 d4; 29.Nc4 Qb5; 30.Qxd4 Bb7; 31.c3 Nb3; 32.Qd3 Bc5; 33.Rd1 h6; 34.Bh4 Ba8; 35.h3 a5; 36.Kh2 a4; 37.Qe2 Bc6; 38.Nd6 Qa5; 39.f5 Qxc3; 40.Be7? 40.Rc2 would maintain an advantage for White.

40...Nc1; 41.Rxc1 Qxc1; 42.Bxf8.

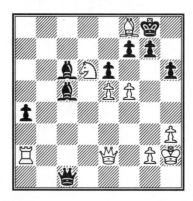

At this point the game was adjourned with resumption set for the next morning. In the interval, Tal had anticipated the sealed move and found **42...Be3!!** The threat is...Bf4+. **43.Kg3 Bg5!; 44.Qc4.** 44.Kf2 Bh4+; 45.g3 Bxg3+; 46.Kxg3 Qg1+; 47.Kf4 Qg5#.

44...Qe3+; 45.Kg4.

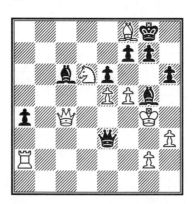

45...Bh4!; 46.Be7. 46.Kxh4 Qg5#. **46...Bxe7; 47.Nxf7 h5+; 48.Kxh5 Be8; 49.Kg4 exf5+; 50.Kxf5 g6+; 51.Kg4 Bd7+. White resigned.**

FIND THE WIN!

(33) TUKMAKOV - TAL
Soviet Championship, 1969

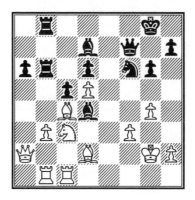

Black is pressing on both wings. Choose the correct flank and Black's killer move.

(34) TAL - MALICH
Varna, 1958

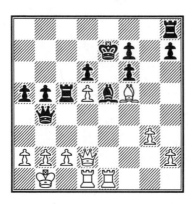

The queens may be exchanged, so White must act desicively.

(35) TAL - PARMA
Bled, 1961

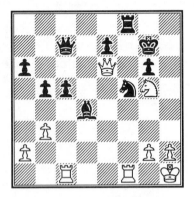

White to move. Liberate a critical square!

(36) TAL - SOLOMIS
Soviet Union, 1970

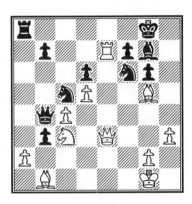

White to move. Black is threatening to capture at a2, and perhaps even make another queen. The kingside, however, belongs to White, if you are quick enough!

12. TIGRAN PETROSIAN

Ninth World Champion (1963–1969)

Petrosian has a reputation as the most positional of World Champions. He was a counterpuncher who would hide behind granite barriers, only to emerge once the opponent had compromised the position by creating a significant weakness. Often, Petrosian would help the process along by investing the exchange in a positional sacrifice. This style did not lend itself to the great quantity of combinations seen in the play of the other World Champions, but he had his share of beauties.

Petrosian excelled at the art of defense. Some of his most interesting combinations were defensive ones, used to wriggle out of a bad position. Most of the rest come from positions where he controlled a great deal of space, which was, paradoxically, the antithesis of his opening strategy, especially as Black.

The following games and exercises show a variety of examples of Petrosian's creative art. His keen eye spotted many beautiful possibilities, and he did his best to lure his opponents into the traps.

(55) AVERBAKH - PETROSIAN
Riga, 1958

We begin with a classic drawing combination. In the days when round robins dominated, the skill of being able to win with White and draw with Black was very useful. During the age of the Swiss System, Black has had to play with more ambition. With the recent trend toward knockout tournaments, this ability will once again play an important role.

1.e4 c5; 2.Nf3 d6; 3.d4 cxd4; 4.Nxd4 Nf6; 5.Nc3 a6; 6.Be2 e5; 7.Nb3 Be7; 8.Be3 0-0; 9.0-0 Be6.

10.f3. A well-known variation has unfolded before us, but at this stage 10.f4 is a more aggressive choice. It seems that Averbakh wanted to support his e4-pawn, in preparation for a siege of the backward d6-pawn, but in Sicilian positions this simple strategy is rarely feasible, since Black has considerable counterplay on the c-file.

10...Nbd7; 11.a4 Qc7; 12.Rf2 Rad8.

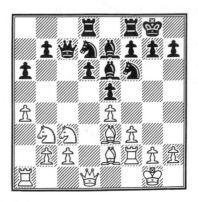

An interesting decision. Rather than reserve this rook for the characteristic Sicilian pressure down the c-file, Petrosian prefers to back up his potential weakness, preparing to eliminate it.

13.a5 Qc6; 14.Bf1 d5; 15.exd5 Bxd5. Why not recapture with the knight? In that case a difficult middle-game could have arisen, but it seems likely that Petrosian was already steering towards the hanging combination which now occurs.

16.Nxd5 Nxd5; 17.Qe1 Nxe3; 18.Qxe3 Nc5; 19.Re2.

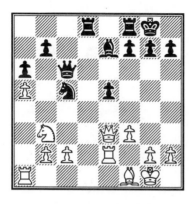

19...Rd3! A startling move which exploits White's vulnerability along the g1–a7 diagonal. Thus 20.cxd3? Nxb3 threatening 21...Nxa1 and 21...Bc5, and **Black wins.** The combination forces a position which has little to build on.

20.Qxe5 Nxb3. Black could consider playing more sharply with 20...Bd6, e.g. 21.Nd4? (or 21.Qf5 Nxb3; 22.cxb3 Rxb3 and the presence of the queens gives Black some pull, since White has weaknesses on both sides of the board.) 21...Qd7 and 22.Qd5 runs into 22...Bxh2+. **21.cxb3 Bf6; 22.Qe4. Draw agreed.** Petrosian could have played on with 22...Qxe4; 23.fxe4 Rxb3 although his winning chances are, by now, remote.

(56) FILIP - PETROSIAN
Yerevan, 1965

Petrosian sets up a King's Indian position by transposition, and enjoys an extra tempo because White wastes time by playing the pawn first to c3, and shortly thereafter advancing it to c4. White nevertheless embarks upon a risky adventure on the kingside, only to open up lines for Petrosian to use on that same flank. The final combination is not only pretty, but rather unusual as well.

1.d4 g6; 2.g3 Bg7; 3.Bg2 c5; 4.c3?! Qc7; 5.Nf3 Nf6; 6.0–0 0–0; 7.b3 d6; 8.Bb2 Nc6; 9.c4 e5; 10.d5. Superior is 10.dxc5 followed by 11.Nc3 with no particular advantage, but at least White is no worse. **10...Na5; 11.Ne1.** More natural is 11.Nc3 and 12.e4.

11...Rb8; 12.Nc2 Bd7; 13.Nd2 Nh5; 14.e4 Bh6; 15.Re1 Rbe8; 16.Ne3 b6.

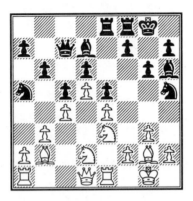

Black is content to maneuver behind the lines. Eventually the f-pawn will be advanced, and the knight will come to the support of the kingside attack from its distant post at a5.

17.Bc3 Ng7; 18.Qe2 f5; 19.exf5 gxf5; 20.Ndf1 Nb7.

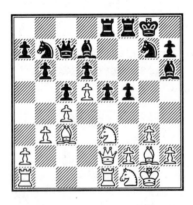

21.g4? The weaknesses are fatal and White's control of e4 is never important. **21...Bxe3!; 22.Nxe3 fxg4; 23.Nxg4.** The kingside has been ripped open, and the Black army rushes in. **23...Qd8; 24.f3 Nh5; 25.Bd2 Nf4; 26.Bxf4 Rxf4; 27.Nf2 Qh4; 28.Ne4 Kh8; 29.Ng3 Nd8.** The knight has plenty of time to join the party by heading to g5.

30.Qf2 Qh6; 31.Re4 Nf7; 32.Kh1 Rf6; 33.Rg1 Ng5; 34.Re3.

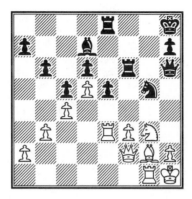

The combination is ready, based on the suffocated position of the White king. Usually the result is a stripping away of the defensive forces. Here, however, most of White's pieces are left on the plate, to be consumed later when the time is right. **34...Qxh2+!** The beautiful culmination of Black's fine positional play. **35.Kxh2 Rh6+; 36.Bh3.** 36.Nh5 Rxh5+; 37.Kg3 Rg8 is a simple win for Black. **36...Nxh3; 37.Nf5.** Objectively, White should play 37.Kg2 Nxf2; 38.Kxf2. **37...Bxf5; 38.Qf1 Nf4+; 39.Kg3 Rg8+; 40.Kf2 Nh3+. White resigned.**

(57) PETROSIAN - LARSEN
Copenhagen, 1960

Larsen's fighting spirit took him to the World Champions candidates stage. He was capable of defeating even the most powerful opponents, but in this encounter early in his career, he runs smack into one of Petrosian's crushing combinations—a classic kingside killer knight sacrifice at f6.

1.Nf3 d6; 2.d4 Nf6; 3.c4 Bg4; 4.Nc3 Nbd7; 5.e4 e5; 6.Be2 Be7; 7.Be3 0-0; 8.0-0 Bh5. A curious move which loses a tempo, much stronger is 8...c6. **9.Nd2 exd4; 10.Bxd4 Bxe2; 11.Qxe2 Re8; 12.f4 Bf8; 13.Rad1 a6; 14.Qf3 c6; 15.g4.**

With the center under control, White's starts a devastating pawn advance. **15...Nc5.** A further error which leads to a strategically lifeless position for him. **16.Bxc5 dxc5; 17.e5 Nd7; 18.Nde4 Qc7; 19.Rd3 Rad8; 20.Rfd1 Nb6; 21.b3 Nc8; 22.g5.** A superb move which prepares the coming sacrifice on f6.

22...Be7; 23.Qh5 Rxd3; 24.Rxd3 Rd8.

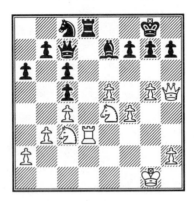

25.Nf6+. The floodgates burst. Perhaps Black had been relying on 25...Bxf6, but that is refuted beautifully as follows: 26.gxf6 Rxd3; 27.Qg5 Kf8; 28.Qgx7 Ke8; 29.Qg8+ Kd7; 30.Qxf7+ Kd8; 31.Qg8+ Kd7; 32.e6+ Kd7; 33.Ne4# or 30...Nd7; 31.e6+! Kc8; 32.fxe7 etc.

25...gxf6; 26.Rh3 Kf8; 27.Qxh7 Ke8; 28.g6. The final key to White's attack. 28...fxg6 fails to 29.e6. **28...Bf8; 29.g7 Bxg7; 30.Qxg7 Qe7; 31.Ne4 Rd1+; 32.Kf2 f5; 33.Nf6+ Kd8; 34.Rh8+. Black resigned.**

(58) LARSEN - PETROSIAN
Santa Monica, 1966

Revenge time, as Larsen delivers a combination of exceptional elegance. Is it too fanciful to suggest that Larsen—consciously or subconsciously—recalled Morphy's famous queen sacrifice at f3, when he sacrificed his own queen against Petrosian's kingside fortifications? Indeed, chess skill is closely related to the ability to recognize and recall patterns. This is why all great chessplayers have studied the classic combination. Themes resurface time and time again at the chessboard.

1.e4 c5; 2.Nf3 Nc6; 3.d4 cxd4; 4.Nxd4 g6; 5.Be3 Bg7; 6.c4 Nf6; 7.Nc3 Ng4; 8.Qxg4 Nxd4; 9.Qd1 Ne6; 10.Qd2 d6; 11.Be2 Bd7; 12.0-0 0-0; 13.Rad1 Bc6; 14.Nd5 Re8. Petrosian starts a series of aimless meanderings which cost four tempi (...Re8/f8; ...Nc7/a6/ c5). Best, of course, is 14...Nc5!, as Larsen should know, since that was played in Porath-Larsen, Amsterdam, 1964.

15.f4 Nc7; 16.f5 Na6; 17.Bg4 Nc5; 18.fxg6 hxg6; 19.Qf2 Rf8.

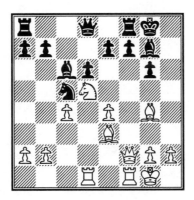

20.e5!! An excellent move which forces Black's minor pieces onto awkward squares. Petrosian has allowed for 20.Bxc5? dxc5; 21.Nf6+ Bxf6; 22.Rxd8 Raxd8 with good compensation for the queen. Black's position is very solid and he would never lose. However, **20...Bxe5; 21.Qh4 Bxd5; 22.Rxd5 Ne6.** Black had much better chances with 22...e6!; 23.Qxd8 Rfxd8; 24.Rxe5 dxe5; 25.Bxc5 and it is not absolutely clear that **White wins.**

23.Rf3 Bf6; 24.Qh6 Bg7.

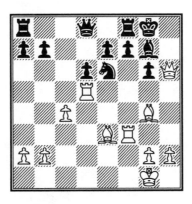

It looks as though White must retreat, but Larsen unleashes a potent combination which reduces Petrosian's kingside to rubble. **25.Qxg6!! Nf4.** The immediate 25...fxg6; 26.Bxe6+ is about the same as this. **26.Rxf4 fxg6; 27.Be6+ Rf7.** Or 27...Kh7; 28.Rh4+ Bh6; 29.Bxh6. **28.Rxf7 Kh8; 29.Rg5 b5; 30.Rg3. Black resigns.** A rare fate for a World Champion.

(59) PETROSIAN - VAITONIS
Saltsjobaden Interzonal, 1952

Petrosian was especially successful on the White side of the Queen's Gambit. There he usually obtained an advantage in space and development, which provided fertile ground for brilliant combinations.

1.d4 Nf6; 2.c4 e6; 3.Nf3 d5; 4.Nc3 Be7; 5.cxd5 exd5; 6.Qc2 0-0; 7.Bg5 Nbd7; 8.e3 c6; 9.Bd3 Re8; 10.0-0 Nf8; 11.Rab1.

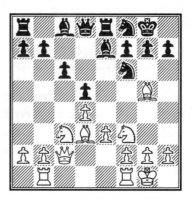

This is the Minority Attack, one of the standard continuations of the Exchange Variation of the Queen's Gambit Declined. White gets ready to use the advance of the a- and b-pawns to undermine the queenside pawn structure. There is another aspect to the position, however. If Black concentrates on defending queenside weaknesses, then the kingside can become vulnerable. Petrosian feints to the left, then slugs his opponent with a blow in the center and finaly begins a brutal assault on the kingside which is assisted by a fine combination.

11...Ne4; 12.Bf4 f5; 13.Ne5 Bf6? A mistake. This square is needed for other things. The knight should have advanced to g6. Black's pieces quickly become disorganized. **14.f3! Nd6; 15.Rbe1 g6.** 15...Ng6; 16.Nxg6 hxg6; 17.g4 would have exposed the weaknesses in Black's kingside.

16.h3 Be6; 17.g4 Rc8; 18.Qh2!

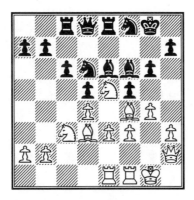

The threat is Nxg6, picking up a pawn since the knight at d6 would be under attack by the White bishop and queen. **18...Be7.** Black should have tried the desperate ...Nc4.

19.Kh1 fxg4? A crucial weakening of the kingside. Now the bishop at d3 can get involved in the attack. 19...g5 would have also been weakening, but Black might have been able to organize a defense with ...Ng6 and ...Rf8.

20.hxg4 Nf7; 21.Nxf7 Bxf7; 22.Be5 Bf6; 23.f4 Bxe5; 24.dxe5 Qe7. 24...d4; 25.Ne4 would have been even worse. **25.Ne2 a6; 26.Nd4.** White's plan is to force through f5, but if the opportunity arises, there is a combination waiting.

26...Ne6.

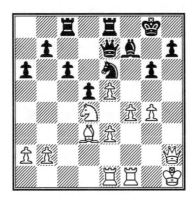

Black's monarch has every reason to be concerned. White is preparing to break through at f5. It is not a pawn that is headed to that square, however. Instead, Petrosian offers a knight, which must be accepted because Black can ill afford to let the knight reach d6. In hindsight, Black should have tried to create counterplay with...c5, which is possible, now that White no longer has access to b5 for the bishop. 26...Nd7 also might have been wiser.

27.Nf5!! gxf5; 28.gxf5 Nf8. The massive pawn front virtually guarantees victory. **29.Rg1+ Kh8; 30.Qh6.**

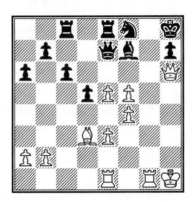

The result of the combination is a decisive advantage. Black offers a knight to soften the blow, but White cuts through the defenses quickly. **30...Ng6.** 30...Bg8; 31.f6 Qc7; 32.Qg7+ Qxg7; 33.fxg7#. **31.fxg6 Bxg6; 32.Rxg6!** White has emerged from the complications with an extra piece. **Black resigned**.

(60) PETROSIAN - PACHMAN
Bled, 1961

Petrosian often deliberately chose cramped positions as White, using such flank openings as the Réti and King's Indian Attack. He would lie in wait, only to leap at any weakness that emerges. In this game, the target is d6.

1.Nf3 c5; 2.g3 Nc6; 3.Bg2 g6; 4.0–0 Bg7; 5.d3 e6; 6.e4 Nge7; 7.Re1 0–0.

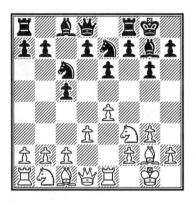

Against the King's Indian Attack, Black must play with care. Pachman now casually castles, an obvious move. This turns out to be a big mistake, however, because White can establish a strong pawn at e5. Therefore 7...d6 was necessary.

8.e5! d6; 9.exd6 Qxd6; 10.Nbd2 Qc7; 11.Nb3 Nd4; 12.Bf4 Qb6; 13.Ne5 Nxb3; 14.Nc4! A little intermezzo that defends b2. **14...Qb5?!** Black should have retreated to d8. **15.axb3.** White keeps the initiative by threatening Ra5.

15...a5; 16.Bd6!

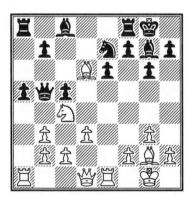

White's minor pieces dominate the board. **16...Bf6; 17.Qf3 Kg7; 18.Re4.** It is hard to criticize this move, but Petrosian has not yet figured out the position. The brilliant combination he uses, next move, could have been played here.

18...Rd8.

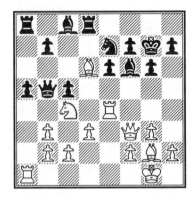

White is ready for action. The dark squares on the kingside invite an invasion, especially with such a monstrous bishop at d6. The only defender is the bishop at f6. **19.Qxf6+!!** White can afford to invest the queen because Black's forces are in no position to defend. The Black queen, bishop and rooks have no useful function. Petrosian may have calculated this to the end, or perhaps simply trusted that his overpowering forces would prevail.

19...Kxf6; 20.Be5+ Kg5.

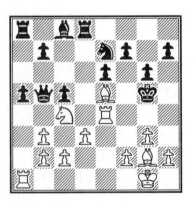

Here we see the touch of a true World Champion. Petrosian has invested a queen for a bishop, but that bishop is very powerful. Indeed, it forces resignation with its next move! **21.Bg7!! Black resigned,** but the rest is not hard to calculate. Black cannot avoid mate in 4. The cutest line is 21...Rxd3; 22.cxd3 Kh5; 23.Rh4+ Kg5; 24.f4+ Kf5; 25.Nd6#.

FIND THE WIN!

(37) PETROSIAN - SPASSKY
World Championship, 1966

Combinational themes can repeat themselves in different guises. Here Petrosian sacrifices his queen on an empty square in order to earn himself a gigantic material advantage. Observant readers will notice that this is the same theme which Alekhine overlooked in his game against Euwe from the 1937 World Championship.

(38) PETROSIAN - IVKOV
USSR - Yugoslavia, 1979

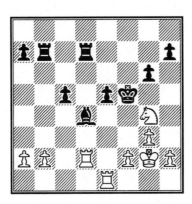

Black's king doesn't have much room to maneuver, and White can exploit this. How?

(39) PETROSIAN - MOLDAGALIYEV
Soviet Union, 1969

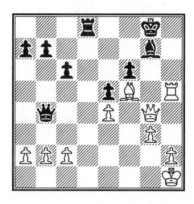

All of White's forces are attacking. Finish the job!

(40) PETROSIAN - STEIN
Soviet Union, 1961

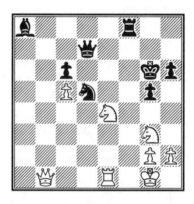

There are plenty of discovered checks, but which one wins?

13. BORIS SPASSKY

Tenth World Champion (1969–1972)

Spassky is known as the guy who lost the crown to Bobby Fischer, breaking the Soviet hegemony on the World Championship. His ascent to the throne gets much less attention these days. This is perhaps due to his inability to maintain his form after that match. While the much older Smyslov was able to make it to the Candidates' Final in 1984, Spassky made only a brief appearance, losing to Anatoly Karpov in his next shot at the title. Since the mid-70's, he has played from time to time but has not presented any serious challenges to modern stars. Even his rematch with Fischer in 1992 ended in his decisive defeat. His greatest games are from the 1950's and 1960's.

Bernard Cafferty, in his collection of Spassky's best games, relates how Spassky explained to him how he was lazy like a Russian Bear, too lazy to bother standing up. At his best, chess seemed to flow through him, seemingly effortlessly. Tremendous complications would lead to combinations that other players couldn't find.

Spassky's contributions to the art of the combination are legendary. His reluctance to write on chess (he is the least prolific of all World Champions) perhaps led to neglect of many of his games, though there are excellent collections of his games by Soltis and Cafferty. Here are some of his finest combinative moments.

(61) SPASSKY - BRONSTEIN
Soviet Championship, 1960

This game contains a combination that has been witnessed by more persons than perhaps any other in chess history. It was featured in the early James Bond film "From Russia With Love," though the names were changed to "Kronstein vs. McAdams." That seems rather cruel, giving the credit to someone with a name similar to that of the loser, but then Spassky, a gentleman, would hardly want to have been associated with the evil Kronstein. The supposed player of the Black pieces was not based on British star, Mickey Adams, who was not born until this film had already become a classic.

1.e4 e5; 2.f4 exf4; 3.Nf3 d5; 4.exd5 Bd6; 5.Nc3 Ne7; 6.d4 0-0; 7.Bd3 Nd7; 8.0-0 h6; 9.Ne4 Nxd5; 10.c4 Ne3; 11.Bxe3 fxe3; 12.c5 Be7; 13.Bc2.

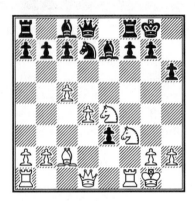

Spassky's combinations are often profound and deep, but at the same time based on very simple observations. In this position, Bronstein is already in trouble, despite the extra pawn. Black's biggest problem is the h7-square. White threatens to play Qd3, followed by moving the knight from e4 and opening the pathway to the checkmating square at h7. Black must defend somehow. Bronstein decides to free the f8-square for the knight, but this weakens the f7-square. **13...Re8; 14.Qd3 e2?** Hoping to deflect the queen to the e-file, where it will be opposed by the rook at e8. The straightforward defense with...Nf8 was preferable. **15.Nd6!!**

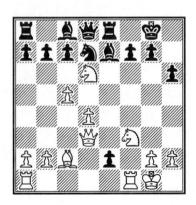

15...Nf8. 15...exf1Q+; 16.Rxf1 Bxd6; 17.Qh7+ Kf8; 18.cxd6 cxd6; 19.Qh8+ Ke7; 20.Re1+ Ne5! was the only defense, though it was hard to calculate and, in any case, Bronstein was short of time. After 21.Qxg7 Rg8!; 22.Qxh6 Qb6; 23.Kh1 Be6; 24.dxe5, White would have enough compensation for the exchange, perhaps, but no more. Does this mean that the combination is completely unsound, or that the sacrifice was not part of a combination at all? We don't think so. Spassky has played the best moves in the positions that have arisen and has sacrificed heavily.

There are further complications and pathways to explore, and we will see that Black missed some chances too. Perhaps this game crosses the border from combination to speculative sacrifice, but is spectacular in either case. **16.Nxf7!!** Clearly, this is the best that White can do, but does it work?

16...exf1Q+; 17.Rxf1.

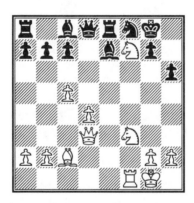

17...Bf5. 17...Kxf7; 18.Ne5+ Kg8; 19.Qh7+ Nxh7; 20.Bb3+ Kh8; 21.Ng6# is a very elegant win for White. 17...Qd5 attracted the attention of many commentators. After a quarter century of analysis, the correct continuation has been established as 18.Bb3! (18.Nxh6+ gxh6; 19.Bb3 Be6; 20.Bxd5 Bxd5 is not better for White.) 18...Qxf7!; 19.Bxf7+ Kxf7.

Black has a rook and two bishops for queen and pawn, but the king is still exposed. Yet Spassky would have had to resist the temptation to leap forward with a discovered check, settling instead for 20.Qc4+ Kg6. (20...Be6; 21.Ng5+ Kg8; 22.Nxe6 Nxe6; 23.Qxe6+ Kh8; 24.Re1 and sooner or later, White will win.) 21.Qg8! Bf6. (21...Be6; 22.Ne5+ Kh5; 23.Qxg7 and it is all over.) 22.Ne5+ Bxe5; 23.Qf7+

Kh7; 24.Qxe8 Bxd4+; 25.Kh1 and Black has three pieces for the queen. But there are still threats to meet, such as Qe4+. 25...Ng6; 26.Rd1 Bxc5; 27.Rd8 Ne7; 28.h4! and Black starts to run out of moves. The simple threat is h5 followed by mate at g8 or h8.

Black offers a bishop to appease Spassky, and the future World Champion is content with the material advantage this confers.

18.Qxf5 Qd7.

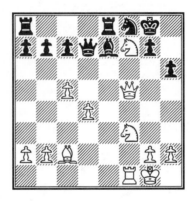

The combination has come to an end. In the aftermath, White has two pieces and a pawn for the rook. The game does not last long. **19.Qf4 Bf6; 20.N3e5 Qe7; 21.Bb3 Bxe5.** 21...Kh7; 22.Qf5+ g6; 23.Qxf6 and there is no point in continuing. **22.Nxe5+ Kh7; 23.Qe4+. Black resigned.**

(62) LARSEN - SPASSKY
Belgrade, 1970

This is a game which was played in the spotlight of a match between the top Soviet stars and players from the rest of the world. This game contains a devastating combination which makes it Spassky's best-known complete game.

1.b3 e5; 2.Bb2 Nc6; 3.c4 Nf6; 4.Nf3. Very risky, 4.e3 is safer. **4...e4; 5.Nd4 Bc5; 6.Nxc6 dxc6.** Sacrificing his pawn-structure for the sake of speedy development, somewhat in the style of Morphy.

7.e3 Bf5; 8.Qc2 Qe7; 9.Be2 0-0-0; 10.f4?! A weakening of White's kingside, but it takes the play of a genius to expose this fault. **10...Ng4; 11.g3 h5; 12.h3 h4!; 13.hxg4 hxg3; 14.Rg1.** Can White's defenses be penetrated?

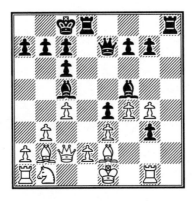

14...Rh1!! The point of this fantastic sacrifice is to seize the h4-square for Black's queen, with tempo. **15.Rxh1 g2; 16.Rf1.** 16.Rg1 Qh4+; 17.Kd1 Qh1! and wins. **16...Qh4+; 17.Kd1 gxf1Q+.** White resigns in view of 18.Bxf1 Bxg4+ mates in, at most, two moves.

(63) SPASSKY - CIRIC
Amsterdam, 1970

1.d4 d5; 2.c4 e6; 3.Nf3 Nf6; 4.g3 Be7; 5.Bg2 0-0; 6.0-0 c6; 7.b3 Nbd7; 8.Bb2 b6; 9.Nbd2 Bb7.

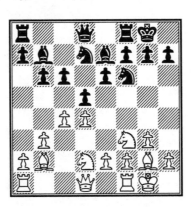

10.Rc1. Spassky opts for the closed form of this opening. We now know that the more aggressive 10.Qc2 should lead nowhere. Ironically, however, Ciric lost a brilliant game as Black in this line to Geller before Black's defense had been properly elaborated.

Geller-Ciric, Oberhausen, 1961, went 10.Qc2 Rc8; 11.Rad1 Qc7; 12.e4 dxe4; 13.Nxe4 Nxe4; 14.Qxe4 c5; 15.d5 Nf6. (15...Bf6!; 16.Qc2 exd5; 17.cxd5 Bxb2; 18.Qxb2 Rcd8; 19.d6 Qb8; 20.Rfe1 Nf6; 21.Re7 Rxd6; 22.Rxd6 Qxd6; 23.Rxb7 Qd1+, as in Geller-Nei, Tiflis, 1967, gives equality.) 16.Qc2 exd5; 17.Be5! Qd8; 18.Ng5 g6; 19.h4 Nh5; 20.Bxd5 Bxd5; 21.Rxd5 Qe8; 22.Re1 Qc6; 23.Bb2 Rfe8; 24.Nxh7! Bxh4; 25.Red1 Qe6; 26.Qc3 f6; 27.Qd3 Qg4; 28.Rg5!! Qe4; 29.Nxf6+ Nxf6; 30.gxh4 Red8; 31.Qxd8+ Rxd8; 32.Rxd8+ Kf7; 33.Bxf6 Kxf6; 34.Rd6+ Kf7; 35.Rdxg6 Qxh4; 36.Rg7+ Kf6!; 37.R7g6+ Kf7; 38.Rg7+ Kf6; 39.R7g6+ Kf7; 40.Rg4 Qh5; 41.Rg7+ Kf6; 42.R4g6+ Kf5; 43.Rg5+ resigns.

10...Rc8; 11.e3 c5; 12.Qe2 Rc7; 13.cxd5 Bxd5. This does not work out very well. Superior is 13...exd5, although this type of position has been known to guarantee White a prolonged initiative since the game Botvinnik-Petrosian, Spartakiad, 1964, the pawn at d5 slightly restricts the scope of Black's b7-bishop, and White gains useful squares for maneuvers-especially e5.

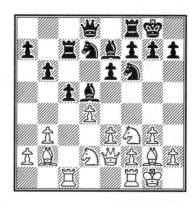

14.e4! Bb7; 15.e5! Nd5; 16.Nc4! Qa8; 17.Nd6!

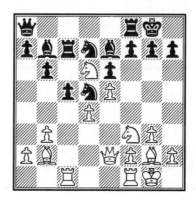

The reader may well question why we have seen fit to adorn Spassky's 14th–17th moves with exclamation marks. Surely they are simple and obvious, so why should they be singled out for particular approval? But it is precisely this quality of being simple and obvious which makes these moves so remarkable.

With nonchalant directness and lack of ceremony, Spassky has established a dominating position. It is usual, in such situations, to continue subtly with the restraint of the center pawns and an attempt to exchange the light-squared bishops, when White may seize an extra square on the queenside, or gain a minute endgame advantage. The disadvantages of ceding the d5 square to a Black knight and of weakening the h1–a8 diagonal are often sufficient to deter White from the advance executed by Spassky in this game. Yet, the then World Champion demonstrates the irrelevance of these considerations. This is a case of "simplicity of means," and it is an excellent example of the concept.

17...Bxd6; 18.exd6 Rc6; 19.dxc5. White can go wrong here in a way which indicates the possible dangers of weakening the h1–a8 diagonal, e.g. the plausible 19.Ne5 Rxd6; 20.Nxd7 Rxd7; 21.dxc5 Nc3; 22.Bxc3 Bxg2; 23.Qe5 f6; 24.Qxe6+ Rdf7, and a drastic twist of fortune has occurred.

19...bxc5. If 19...Rxc5, White really could play 20.Ne5, undermining the position of the c5-rook and the d7-Knight, enhancing the power of the d6-pawn and clearing a path towards g7, e.g. 20...Nxe5; 21.Rxc5 bxc5; 22.Qxe5. Black has no way to organizing a counter-blow along the h1–a8 diagonal in this line.

20.Ng5. Playing for mate. White abandons the d6-pawn as a decoy, quite in the style of Alekhine. **20...Rxd6; 21.Rfd1 Ra6; 22.Qe4 f5.** An unfortunate necessity, since the d5-Knight is pinned. But now White can fasten onto another weakness.

23.Qc4 Qe8; 24.Re1.

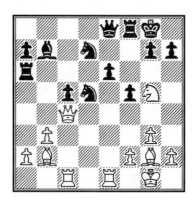

24...Rxa2. Hubris? Or was Ciric willfully co-operating to create a beautiful finish? Such acts of aesthetic generosity and public-spiritedness are not unknown when a player realizes his position is beyond redemption. **25.Rxe6 Qa8; 26.Bxd5 Bxd5; 27.Qh4.** The shifts of front, by the White queen, are an especially attractive feature of this outstandingly beautiful game.

27...h6; 28.Qxh6 Nf6; 29.Rxf6. Black resigned. 29...Rxf6; 30.Qh7+ Kf8; 31.Qh8+ Bg8; 32.Bxf6 gxf6; 33.Qxf6+ Ke8; 34.Re1+ Kd7; 35.Re7+ is convincing. This scherzando finish is a fine indication of the combinative artistry of which the flank debuts are capable. Its simplicity and concentrated force are, in my opinion, infinitely more satisfying than the stereotyped "brilliancies" which are manufactured from the "combinational workshop" of such openings as the Morra, Göring and Wing Gambits or the Blackmar-Diemer.

(64) BARDA - SPASSKY
Bucharest, 1953

Unlike his predecessors, Boris Spassky can not be easily described in terms of a special style. Spassky was the first great universal player, as comfortable in massive complications as in quiet positional waters. In this early game he shows great maturity, patiently accumulating positional advantages in a manner which would impress Steinitz himself. Then, he unleashes a Tal-like combination in a display of raw aggression.

1.d4 Nf6; 2.Nf3 c5; 3.d5 g6; 4.g3 Bg7; 5.Bg2 0–0; 6.0-0 d6; 7.h3 b5; 8.a4 Bb7; 9.Nh2 a6; 10.axb5 axb5; 11.Rxa8 Bxa8.

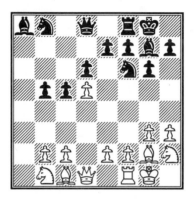

Black's position contains some venom. The plan involves an invasion of White's position from the flank, specifically via the a-file.

12.Na3 Qd7; 13.b3 Na6; 14.Bb2 Nc7; 15.e4 Bb7; 16.Qe2 Ra8; 17.Bc1 Ra7; 18.f4.

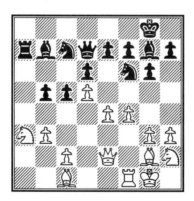

Spassky notices that both White knights are in terrible positions. Although White seems to dominate the center, a standard Benoni break is now employed to transform White's dynamic center into a fixed formation.

18...e6!; 19.c4 b4; 20.Nc2 exd5; 21.exd5 Ra2; 22.g4.

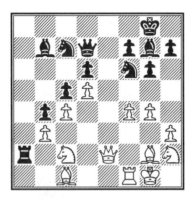

The invasion has begun. White is trying to create some counterplay on the kingside, but Black has nothing to worry about there. What is surprising, though, is that the seemingly powerful pawn at d5 turns out to be vulnerable after all!

22...Nfxd5!! This is the start of a combination that nets a rook and three pawns for two minor pieces. The combination is based on another insight by Spassky—the fact that the queen at e2 is overworked, having to defend both d5 and c2!

23.cxd5 Ba6; 24.Qd1 Bxf1; 25.Bxf1? If 25.Nxf1, then 25...Nb5 and Black has a strong game, but after 26.Qd3 Nc3; 27.Nf3 Black has no tangible advantage. This resource was missed by Grandmaster commentators, but found by 13-year old Master Vinay Bhat!

Nxd5; 26.Qxd5 Rxc2; 27.Be3.

The fireworks have ended. Black's position is already winning. White's forces are scattered and there are weaknesses on the back three ranks. Naturally Spassky would like to get queens off the board, to prevent any attack based on, for example, Bc4 and Nf3-g5. **27...Qe6!; 28.Qa8+ Bf8; 29.Bf2 Qxb3.** White has avoided the exchange of queens, but Black threatens to get an additional queen soon. **30.g5 Rc1; 31.Kg2 Qa3; 32.Qd5 Ra1; 33.Ng4 Qa8!** Now the queens come off, and the endgame is simple. **34.Bc4 Bg7; 35.Qxa8+ Rxa8; 36.Nf6+ Bxf6; 37.gxf6 Ra3; 38.Be1 b3; 39.Bc3 Ra2+; 40.Kf3 Rc2. White resigned.**

(65) SPASSKY - TAIMANOV
Soviet Championship, 1955

We have already remarked how dangerous it is to delay castling against a top caliber opponent. Spassky punishes one of the best players of the day, using deceptively simple moves, in a manner reminiscent of Smyslov.

1.e4 e5; 2.Nf3 Nc6; 3.Bb5 a6; 4.Ba4 b5; 5.Bb3 Na5; 6.0–0 d6; 7.d4 Nxb3; 8.axb3 f6.

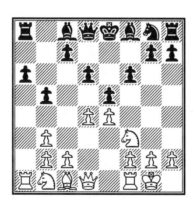

Black has adopted a rather artificial variation of the Spanish Game. Spassky continues with development, but the advance of the c-pawn to c4 might have been stronger.

9.Nc3 Bb7; 10.Nh4 Ne7; 11.dxe5 dxe5; 12.Qf3 Qd7; 13.Rd1 Qe6. The queen sits comfortably here, where it can keep an eye on the center and can retreat to f7 in the event of a check at h5. Spassky sees, however, that the f7-square is not as secure as it seems.

14.Be3 g5.

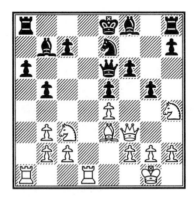

This is an open invitation to disaster. Spassky uses a combination to win the queen. Black will temporarily have material compensation, but the Black position is so weak that White will soon win additional pawns.

15.Nxb5! axb5; 16.Qh5+ Qf7; 17.Rxa8+ Bxa8; 18.Rd8+! Kxd8; 19.Qxf7 gxh4; 20.Qxf6.

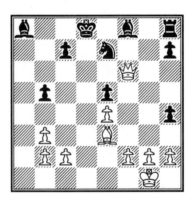

Black has a rook, bishop, and knight for a queen and two pawns, but virtually every one of Black's pieces is in a vulnerable position and the forces are uncoordinated. **20...Rg8; 21.f3 h3; 22.g3 Ke8; 23.Qxe5 Rg6; 24.Qxb5+ Bc6; 25.Qb8+ Kf7; 26.Qxc7.** White has gobbled up three pawns and wins without difficulty. **26...Rf6; 27.Bg5 Re6; 28.b4 Kg8; 29.Qb8 Ng6; 30.Kf2 Ne5; 31.b5 Be8; 32.Be3 Bd6; 33.Qc8 Kf7; 34.b6 Rf6; 35.Bf4 Bd7; 36.b7 Be6; 37.Bxe5 Bxe5; 38.b8Q Bxc8; 39.Qxc8. Black resigned.**

(66) SPASSKY - BILEK
Moscow, 1967

The White side of the Sicilian was Spassky's favorite opening, and on the way to the World Championship he scored an amazing 75% against it. The opening presents many opportunities for combinations, and when Black leaves the king in the center, punishment could be swift.

1.e4 c5; 2.Nf3 d6; 3.d4 cxd4; 4.Nxd4 Nf6; 5.Nc3 Nc6; 6.Bg5 Bd7; 7.Qd2 a6; 8.0–0–0 Rc8; 9.f4 h6; 10.Bxf6 gxf6; 11.Be2 h5; 12.Kb1 e6; 13.Rhf1 b5; 14.Nxc6 Rxc6; 15.Bf3 Rc5; 16.f5.

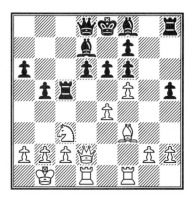

This is a typical Sicilian of the Richter-Rauzer or Najdorf variety. Black's king is stuck in the center, but protected by a wall of pawns. The open c-file gives Black some hopes of a queenside attack. Black should now play conservatively with the queen at c7, defending d6 while adding pressure to the c-file.

16...Qa5?!; 17.fxe6 fxe6; 18.e5! A surprising move. White offers the e-pawn three different ways, but Black has only one option that does not get punished immediately. **18...Rxe5.** 18...fxe5? lets White infiltrate with 19.Qg5!

19.Qf4 Rf5; 20.Qg3 Rg5; 21.Qh4 d5.

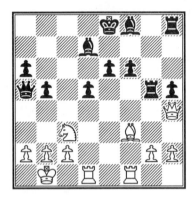

Now the combinational fireworks explode! The king in the center is a juicy target. **22.Bxd5!! exd5; 23.Rxf6.** White will win the d-pawn too, since Black must defend the rook at g5 whose protector has just been eliminated.

23...Rhg8. 23...Rg4 loses quickly to 24.Re1+ Be7; 25.Rxe7+!! Kxe7; 26.Nxd5+! Ke8. (26...Kd8; 27.Rf8#.) 27.Re6+! and the queen gets to e7, with mate to follow. **24.Nxd5 Bg4.** This is the best defense, in that it forces White to find a good move. **25.Rxf8+!** and here **Black resigned.**

White wins because of the weakness of the e7-square, for example; 25...Kxf8; 26.Rf1+ Ke8; 27.Nf6+ followed by Nxg8.

FIND THE WIN!

(41) SPASSKY, - PFLEGER
Munich, 1979

Find the weak spot in Black's fortress.

(42) SPASSKY - SMYSLOV
Bucharest, 1953

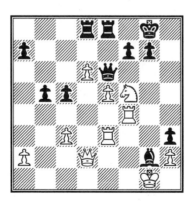

Black's pieces are in no position to defend the king, so rush in!

(43) SPASSKY - AVERKIN
Soviet Union, 1973

White to move. To figure this one out, just concentrate on the dark squares.

(44) SPASSKY - DARGA
Varna Olympiad, 1962

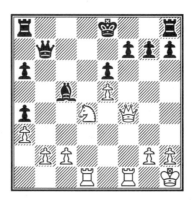

The White king rests safely at h1, while there is an imposing presence of the White rooks on key open files. Their enemy counterparts are on their home squares. Exploit this to win.

14. ROBERT FISCHER

Eleventh World Champion (1972–1975)

To many, Bobby Fischer is the epitome of a World Champion. Moody, brilliant, more than a little paranoid and simply awesome at the chess board. He has only played one serious competition since his 1975 refusal to defend his World Championship title, pummeling Boris Spassky in 1992. It is his refusal to play, more than anything else, that has reduced his chances of being remembered as the greatest player of all time.

Kasparov once said of Fischer that even more than other World Champions, Fischer simply didn't make many bad moves. Robert Burger, in *The Chess of Bobby Fischer*, observed that Fischer "sees more combinations inherent in moves, seizes upon them more often, and pursues them more accurately in their proper sequence of moves—than any other player alive." Most of Fischer's opponents seem to have found ways to make bad moves which allowed nice combinations, but this is just a result of Fischer's avoidance of bad moves.

To select a few of Fischer's brilliant combinations is no easy task. There are plenty of examples at all stages of the game. We have chosen a few which capture his particularly effective style, covering the entire span of his career to date.

(67) BYRNE - FISCHER
US Championship, NY, 1963

The miraculous nature of this game is demonstrated quite clearly by the fact that many people simply refused to believe in it! When White resigned, a number of spectating Grandmasters could not understand why (!!), while a controversy raged for over a year afterwards as to the soundness of Fischer's combination, which was, in fact, ultimately vindicated.

1.d4 Nf6; 2.c4 g6; 3.g3 c6; 4.Bg2 d5; 5.cxd5 cxd5; 6.Nc3 Bg7;
7.e3?! 0–0; 8.Nge2 Nc6; 9.0–0 b6; 10.b3 Ba6; 11.Ba3 Re8; 12.Qd2.

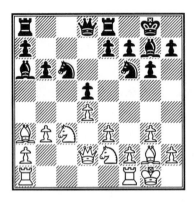

12...e5! Whether "sound" or not, this move is justified on the
grounds that it sets White a multitude of problems. As it is, the
move is sound. **13.dxe5 Nxe5; 14.Rfd1.** If 14.Rad1, then Fischer
would have played 14...Qc8!
14...Nd3.

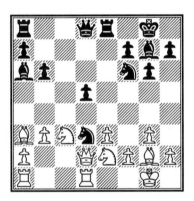

15.Qc2. It was later claimed that 15.Nf4 would have refuted
Fischer's play, but Fischer refuted the "refutation" with 15...Ne4!
**15...Nxf2!!; 16.Kxf2 Ng4+; 17.Kg1 Nxe3; 18.Qd2 Nxg2; 19.Kxg2
d4!; 20.Nxd4 Bb7+; 21.Kf1 Qd7! White resigned.**

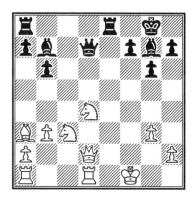

Byrne clearly saw what the spectators had missed: 22.Qf2 Qh3+; 23.Kg1 Re1+; 24.Rxe1 Bxd4 and the threat of mate on g2 costs White the queen. 22.Ndb5 Qh3+; 23.Kg1 Bh6 also wins.

(68) FISCHER - BENKO
United States Championship, 1963

This one is short and sweet. It contains an amazing combination which demonstrates Fischer's efficiency. He finds a way to squelch all counterplay, and finishes the game in style.

1.e4 g6; 2.d4 Bg7; 3.Nc3 d6; 4.f4 Nf6; 5.Nf3 0–0; 6.Bd3 Bg4?!; 7.h3 Bxf3; 8.Qxf3 Nc6?!; 9.Be3 e5; 10.dxe5! dxe5; 11.f5 gxf5; 12.Qxf5 Nd4; 13.Qf2 Ne8; 14.0–0 Nd6; 15.Qg3 Kh8; 16.Qg4! c6; 17.Qh5 Qe8? 17...Ne6 would have been more solid.

18.Bxd4 exd4.

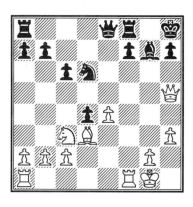

Now Fischer unleashes one of his most famous tactical moves. Since 19.e5 would be met by 19...f5, he eliminates that possibility in the bluntest, yet most unexpected, manner. **19.Rf6!!** The rook must not be captured because then 20.e5! would win. **19...Kg8; 20.e5 h6; 21.Ne2!** There is no defense, so **Black resigned.**

(69) FISCHER - SPASSKY
Sveti Stefan (match), 1992

The rematch between Fischer and Spassky, 20 years after their first encounter, was an interesting affair. Fischer showed some evidence of his old form in the present game. In truly modern style, however, most of the advantage he obtained was a result of home preparation.

1.e4 e5; 2.Nf3 Nc6; 3.Bb5 a6; 4.Bxc6 dxc6; 5.0-0 f6; 6.d4 exd4; 7.Nxd4 c5; 8.Nb3 Qxd1; 9.Rxd1 Bg4; 10.f3 Be6; 11.Nc3 Bd6; 12.Be3 b6; 13.a4.

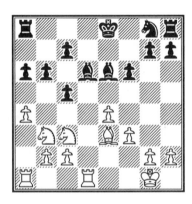

The opening has followed a path that had been recommended for Black by many theoréticians. The approved continuation, before this game, was queenside castling, which Spassky would soon discover to be flawed. A key positional factor is the ability of White's pawn to advance to a5. Black should have prevented this with 13...a5.

13...0-0-0. The books said this was a fine move, but Fischer proves otherwise. **14.a5 Kb7; 15.e5!** A small pseudo-sacrifice, which is part of a prepared plan by Fischer. **15...Be7.** 15...fxe5; 16.axb6 cxb6; 17.Ne4 Bc7 invites another sacrifice: 18.Nbxc5+ bxc5; 19.Nxc5+ Kc8; 20.Rxd8+ Bxd8; 21.Nxe6 and White wins at least another pawn.

16.Rxd8 Bxd8; 17.Ne4.

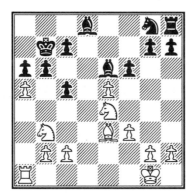

Fischer had done his homework well. There is nothing new here, but Spassky was clearly not familiar with the theory of this particular variation. **17...Kc6?** 17...Bxb3; 18.cxb3 f5; 19.Rd1 Ne7; 20.Ng5 Nc6; 21.axb6 Bxg5; 22.Bxg5 Kxb6; 23.Rd7 Re8; 24.Rxg7 Rxe5; 25.Rxh7 Re1+; 26.Kf2 Rb1; 27.h4 was a 1980 game played by Fischer's friend Peter Biyiasas as White.

18.axb6 cxb6.

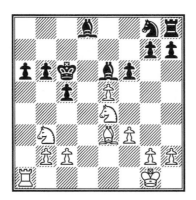

We are in an endgame, where combinations are not all that common. In a sense, however, Black has not completed the opening stage of the game, as the kingside pieces are still undeveloped. This allows White to create a combination. **19.Nbxc5! Bc8.** 19...bxc5; 20.Rxa6+ Kd7; 21.Nxc5+ Ke7; 22.Nxe6 g6; 23.Bc5+ Ke8; 24.Ra8 and the bishop falls. **20.Nxa6 fxe5; 21.Nb4+. Black resigned.**

(70) SAIDY - FISCHER
New York, 1965

Here Fischer takes advantage of his understanding of the endgame to build a winning combination involving liquidation of pieces. This is a classic technique, but it requires precise evaluation of the resulting endgame position.

1.c4 Nf6; 2.Nc3 e6; 3.d4 Bb4; 4.e3 b6; 5.Nge2 Ba6; 6.Ng3 Bxc3+; 7.bxc3 d5; 8.Qf3 0–0; 9.e4 dxc4; 10.Bg5 h6; 11.Bd2 Nbd7; 12.e5 Nd5; 13.Nf5 exf5; 14.Qxd5 Re8; 15.Bxc4.

From all appearances White is on the attack, with tremendous pressure at f7. Yet in reality, the attack involves too little force. Fischer sees the White rooks lying helplessly in their cubby holes and uses a combination to lead to an endgame where, even though he remains behind in material, he can count on a decisive advantage. **15...Nxe5!; 16.Qxd8 Nxc4+!** The tactic of discovered check forces White to give up the queen for the rook at e8.

17.Qxe8+ Rxe8+; 18.Kd1 Nxd2; 19.Kxd2 Re2+; 20.Kc1 Rxf2.

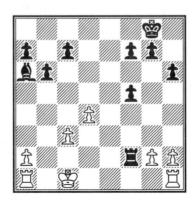

The combination has led to an endgame where White has an extra exchange for two pawns, but the rooks have no useful functions and the domination of the seventh rank cannot be contested. **21.g3 Bb7; 22.Re1 Be4!** Black closes the only open file before dining on the pawns. **23.Re3 Rxh2.** It was an easy matter to exploit the massive advantage on the kingside. **24.a4 h5; 25.Ra3 g5; 26.Rb3 f6; 27.a5 h4; 28.axb6 axb6; 29.gxh4 Rxh4; 30.Ra3 Rh7; 31.Ra7 Re7; 32.d5 Kf7; 33.Kd2 f4; 34.Re1 f5; 35.c4 g4; 36.Rb7 g3; 37.d6 cxd6; 38.Rxb6 f3.** White resigned.

(71) FISCHER - BOLBOCHAN
Stockholm Interzonal , 1962

The Sicilian Defense often gives rise to combinations, since the players often castle on opposite sides of the board. Getting to the king is paramount, and material cannot be spared in the quest. Like his predecessor, Spassky, Fischer loved to play the White side of the Sicilian. But he also relied almost exclusively on the Sicilian as his defense to 1.e4! The combinational possibilities for both sides were, no doubt, part of the attraction. This game has been particularly controversial, in that analysts have tried to "correct" Fischer's own notes. We shall see that this venture has met with mixed results.

1.e4 c5; 2.Nf3 d6; 3.d4 cxd4; 4.Nxd4 Nf6; 5.Nc3 a6; 6.h3 Nc6; 7.g4 Nxd4; 8.Qxd4 e5; 9.Qd3 Be7; 10.g5 Nd7; 11.Be3.

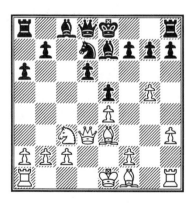

Here Black must acquiesce to the endgame that is likely to arise after exchanges at g5 and e7. **11...Nc5?** 11...Bxg5; 12.Bxg5 Qxg5; 13.Qxd6 Qe7; 14.Qxe7+ Kxe7; 15.Nd5+ Kf8; 16.0-0-0 g6 was suggested by Kotov. Black is still fighting for equality after, for example: 17.f3 b5; 18.Rh2 followed by doubling rooks on the d-file. Nevertheless, this continuation is superior to that of the game. **12.Qd2 Be6; 13.0-0-0 0-0; 14.f3 Rc8; 15.Kb1.** A typical Sicilian position. Black will attack on the queenside with the queen, rook, light-squared bishop and knight. Strangely, Bolbochan retreats the knight here.

15...Nd7; 16.h4 b5; 17.Bh3 Bxh3; 18.Rxh3 Nb6; 19.Bxb6 Qxb6; 20.Nd5.

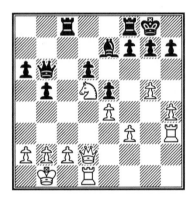

White has a dominating position. There is the possibility of exchanging at e7 and winning the pawn at d6. **20...Qd8; 21.f4!?** Fischer does not fall for the trap: 21.Nxe7+?! Qxe7 where 22.Qxd6?? loses instantly to 22...Rfd8; and the weakness of the back rank is fatal to White. We think that 21.Rg1 would have achieved similar results without allowing the amount of counterplay Bolbochan achieves in the game.

21...exf4; 22.Qxf4 Qd7; 23.Qf5 Rcd8; 24.Ra3! Qa7; 25.Rc3 Fischer could have chosen the more speculative 25.Nf6+!? but after 25...Bxf6! (25...gxf6?; 26.gxf6 Kh8; 27.Qg5 Rg8; 28.fxe7!) 26.gxf6 g6, Black's position is not necessarily hopeless. 27.Qg5 Kh8 White can pick off the queenside pawns. 28.Qxb5 Qf2; 29.Rxa6. Perhaps Fischer considered that the queenside pawns would be hard to advance, and that after 29...Qxf6 Black would have less to worry about on the kingside. 25.Nxe7+ Qxe7; 26.Rxa6 Rfe8; 27.a4!

25...g6! The only defense. Still, now the dark squares are vulnerable. **26.Qg4 Qd7; 27.Qf3 Qe6; 28.Rc7 Rde8.** This locks in the rook at f8, but there was nothing better, for example 28...Rd7 loses to 29.Nf4. 28...Rfe8; 29.Rf1 completely ties down Black's position. 28...Rc8; 29.Ra7 Ra8; 30.Rxa8 Rxa8; 31.Nc7 forks the queen and rook. **29.Nf4 Qe5; 30.Rd5 Qh8; 31.a3 h6; 32.gxh6 Qxh6.** 32...Bxh4? loses elegantly to 33.Nxg6! fxg6; 34.Qb3 Rf7; 35.Rf5 and f7 falls.

33.h5 Bg5.

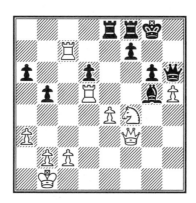

The combination that follows is remarkable. White walks into a pin on the f-file and gives up the knight at f4. **34.hxg6! fxg6.** 34...Bxf4 leads to a hopeless endgame. 35.gxf7+ Rxf7; 36.Rxf7 Kxf7; 37.Rh5! and White recovers the bishop, while keeping the heat on the enemy king. 37...Qg6; 38.Qxf4+ Ke7; 39.Rh6 Qg1+; 40.Ka2 and now White will be able to set up a winning endgame, for example: 40...Qc5; 41.Qf6+ Kd7; 42.Rh7+ Kc8 (42...Kc6; 43.Qf7 Qc4+; 44.Qxc4+ bxc4). 43.Qf7 and Black must play 43...Qc4+; 44.Qxc4 bxc4 when 45.Ra7 wins.

35.Qb3!

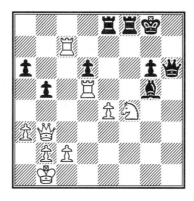

35...Rxf4. Declining the offer doesn't work either. 35...Bxf4?? allows 36.Rh5+! Much more interesting is 35...Kh8; 36.Nxg6+!! Qxg6; 37.Rxg5!! Rf1+ (37...Qxg5; 38.Qh3+ Kg8; 39.Qh7#.) 38.Ka2 Qxg5; 39.Qh3+ Kg8; 40.Qxf1 Qg6; 41.Qf5 leads to a winning endgame.

We must pause here, just before the end of the game, and mention that the new edition of Fischer's *My 60 Memorable Games*, edited by John Nunn, actually replaced the winning line given at move 40 with the erroneous 40.Qh7+ Kf8; 41.Qh8+ Qg8; 42.Qh6+ Qg7; 43.Qxg7#. But, in fact, this "correction" fails, and in fact, isn't even legal, since 41...Qg8 is a check! The line does not win for White!

This should be a warning to all analysts who think they can do better than the players themselves, though we must point out that in the vast majority of cases, as we saw in Réti-Alekhine notes, Nunn's corrections in analysis are improvements. The controversy swirling around his editing of Fischer's notes is that there, unlike his editions of other works, the changes are presented as if they were Fischer's own words, and not in footnotes clearly indicating Nunn's opinions. **36.Re5+! Kf8; 37.Rxe8+. Black resigned.** White infiltrates with Qe6+ and mates quickly.

(72) KRAMER - FISCHER,
United States Championship, 1957

In this next example, a young Bobby Fischer shows his tactical prowess with a double sacrifice as part of a knockout combination.

1.Nf3 Nf6; 2.g3 g6; 3.Bg2 Bg7; 4.d3 d6; 5.0–0 0–0; 6.e4 c5; 7.c3 Nc6; 8.Ne1?! The start of a very passive plan.

8...Rb8!

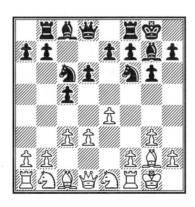

The contour of the middlegame is set. Black takes the initiative and is prepared to blast open the queenside, a typical strategy in the Closed Sicilian we have reached by transposition.

9.f4 Ne8; 10.Be3 Bd7; 11.Nd2 b5; 12.e5? dxe5; 13.Bxc5 exf4; 14.Rxf4 Nc7; 15.Rf1 b4! 16.Qc2 bxc3; 17.bxc3 Nb5; 18.d4 Rc8! 19.Qb2.

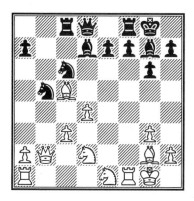

White has an awkward position, but the center seems solid enough. Appearances can be deceiving, however. **19...Nxc3!** The base of the pawn chain falls. **20.Qxc3 Nxd4!!** Fantastic! A second knight is offered. White cannot accept, because the bishop is pinned.

21.Qb4. 21.Qxd4 Bxd4+; 22.Bxd4 Bb5; 23.Rf4 e5! is yet another exploitation of the pin. **21...Ne2+; 22.Kh1 Rxc5!; 23.Qxc5 Bxa1.**

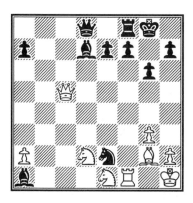

White is down two pawns, and Fischer won without difficulty. **24.Nef3 Bg7; 25.Re1 Nc3; 26.Qxa7 Be6; 27.a3 Qd6; 28.Qa5 Bd5; 29.Nb1? Ra8!; 30.Qb4 Qxb4; 31.axb4 Bxf3; 32.Nxc3 Bxg2+. White resigned.**

FIND THE WIN!

(45) FISCHER - DELY
Skopje, 1967

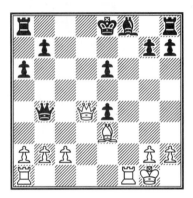

Here, there are distinct similarities with position number 44. You need to sacrifice not just material, but one of your positional assets as well.

(46) FISCHER - MIAGMASUREN
Sousse Interzonal, 1967

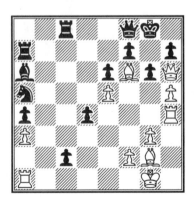

Finish quickly, but with style.

(47) BISGUIER - FISCHER
New York, 1960

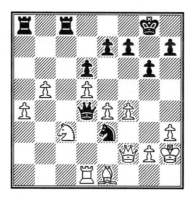

This position looks complicated since the White, passed pawns are dangerous, but Fischer brutally eliminates all resistance.

(48) CARDOSO - FISCHER
New York (match), 1957

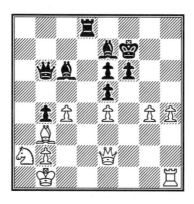

Fischer is a pawn down, but he regains it with interest.

15. ANATOLY KARPOV

Twelfth World Champion
(1975-1985 and FIDE World Champion 1993–present)

Karpov is known as one of the greatest positional players of all time, and his preference for quiet positions has characterized his style ever since he was awarded the World Championship title after Bobby Fischer refused to defend it in 1975. Therefore, his combinational output is much smaller than that of the other World Champions. Karpov's wins tend to involve the steady accumulation of advantages and exploitation of opponent errors.

His ability to calculate is strong, but from time to time he will lose concentration and has committed some whopping blunders. When focused, he excels at defense, and his success is due in no small part to his ability to anticipate enemy plans. Karpov does not take risks. He enters complications, usually, only after he has worked out all the details. A sharper style emerged in his 1998 FIDE World Championship match against Viswanathan Anand, though he did make some serious tactical errors in his successful title defense.

Karpov has held the FIDE World Championship for most of the last quarter of the 20th century. He has been eclipsed by Garry Kasparov, who took the FIDE title from him in 1985, and abandoned it in favor of the PCA crown in 1993. He remains one of the most active champions, and continues to produce artistic games, and, from time to time, a memorable and instructive combination. Some of his artistry is displayed in the following examples.

(73) KARPOV - KORCHNOI
Moscow USSR, 1974

Karpov has no fear of complicated openings. In this game, from the Candidates final that was to earn him the World Championship, he enters one of the most uncompromising openings of all, the mighty Dragon, and finds a brilliant combination waiting.

1.e4 c5; 2.Nf3 d6; 3.d4 cxd4; 4.Nxd4 Nf6; 5.Nc3 g6; 6.Be3 Bg7; 7.f3 Nc6; 8.Qd2 0-0; 9.Bc4 Bd7; 10.h4 Rc8; 11.Bb3 Ne5; 12.0-0-0 Nc4; 13.Bxc4 Rxc4; 14.h5 Nxh5; 15.g4 Nf6.

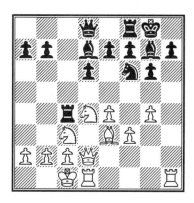

This has been well-known theory for a long time, and is a typical Yugoslav Attack in the Dragon Sicilian, which has seen more than its fair share of combinations from both sides of the board.

16.Nde2. This is an excellent move. It consolidates the position of the knight at c3, and eliminates any Black notion of an exchange sacrifice at c3. It is interesting to note that Karpov takes time out for safety right in the middle of his fierce attack on the kingside. This sort of move underlines the contrast between modern players and the old Masters. You would not find Morphy or Anderssen taking time out for such preliminaries.

16...Qa5; 17.Bh6 Bxh6; 18.Qxh6 Rfc8; 19.Rd3.

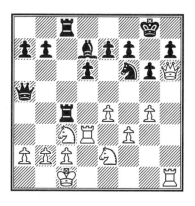

This is the perfect companion to Karpov's 16th move. Now the threat of g5 looms large. Korchnoi had probably analyzed this at home, but not as deeply as Karpov. He took a long time to respond to this move, perhaps noticing some flaws in his preparation.

19...R4c5; 20.g5! The beginning of a long and brilliant combination. **20...Rxg5.** Black accepts the pawn. However, the last chance to resist was 20...Nh5. Here is one example: 20...Nh5; 21.Nf4 Rxc3; 22.Rxc3 Rxc3; 23.Nxh5! gxh5; 24.Qxh5! Kf8; 25.Qh6+ Ke8; 26.Qxh7 and White threatens Qh8+ followed by Qxc3, so Black has to try the desperate 26...Rxc2+; 27.Kxc2 Be6. But after 28.Qg8+ Kd7; 29.a3 Qb5, that turns out to be good enough for a draw. **21.Rd5 Rxd5; 22.Nxd5 Re8; 23.Nef4.** White's knight, which had been overprotecting c3, now returns to the attack with decisive force.

23...Bc6.

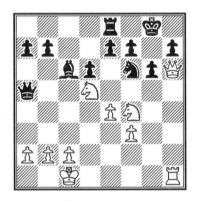

23...Be6; 24.Nxe6 fxe6; 25.Nxf6+ exf6; 26.Qxh7+ Kf8; 27.Qxb7 and White cleans up quickly. **24.e5!** This must have been the most difficult move to find. It jams the route to g5, short-circuiting Black's resistance. 24.Nxf6+ exf6; 25.Nh5! Qg5+!; 26.Qxg5 fxg5; 27.Nf6+ Kf8; 28.Nxe8 Kxe8; 29.Rxh7 f5 and Black can continue to resist. **24...Bxd5; 25.exf6 exf6; 26.Qxh7+ Kf8; 27.Qh8+. Korchnoi resigned.**

This beautiful game has been showered with praise and prizes by journalists the world over, as well as by the judges at the competition. But there is a troubling question. Was this really a game, or did Korchnoi merely stumble down the paths of pre-game analysis by Karpov and his seconds, Geller and Furman? We know that much of it was preparation, and the speed with which Karpov executed his plan indicates that this may all have been home cooking, as in the case of Kasparov's demolition of Viswanathan Anand that we will see later on. Of what sporting, rather than scientific, value is a combination conceived at home in the laboratory, or now, with the assistance of computers? It is as if a favorite painting, supposedly from the brush of a great artist, turned out, on closer inspection, to be a forgery by numbers!

(74) TIMMAN - KARPOV
Montreal, 1979

Karpov is not known for aggressive play, especially as Black. In this game, however, he aims his pieces at White's kingside and fires away. The result is a brilliant combination.

1.c4 Nf6; 2.Nc3 e5; 3.Nf3 Nc6; 4.e3 Be7; 5.d4 exd4; 6.Nxd4 0–0; 7.Nxc6 bxc6; 8.Be2 d5; 9.0–0 Bd6; 10.b3 Qe7; 11.Bb2 dxc4; 12.bxc4 Rb8; 13.Qc1 Ng4; 14.g3 Re8; 15.Nd1.

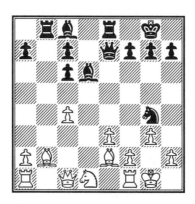

White has played without energy and has a passive position. The king is defended only by the bishop at e2 and rook at f1, and this allows Black to sacrifice material to launch a combination.

15...Nxh2! The target is actually g3. The defender at h2 is gone. **16.c5.** Inventive counterplay, attacking the bishop at d6 which needs to remain on the b8-h2 diagonal. Taking the knight gets clobbered. 16.Kxh2? Qh4+; 17.Kg1 Bxg3; 18.fxg3 Qxg3+; 19.Kh1 Re4 and White is in serious trouble. The best try is 20.Rf4 Qe1+; 21.Kg2 Qxe2+; 22.Kg3 Rxb2; 23.Qxb2 (23.Nxb2 Re5! and there is no defense to mate in 4!) 23...Rxe3+; 24.Nxe3 Qxb2; 25.Rd1 g5! and Black has three extra pawns, with more coming. 19...Re6 is not as good, since Black can hang on with 20.Bf6 Rxf6; 21.Rxf6 Qh4+; 22.Kg1 Qxf6.

16...Nxf1; 17.cxd6.

What now? Black's queen, knight and pawns on the c-file are all under attack, and White may take the initiative with Qc3? How does the combination continue? With another sacrifice!

17...Nxg3!!; 18.fxg3. 18.dxe7 Nxe2+; 19.Kf1 Nxc1; 20.Bxc1 Rxe7 gives Black an extra exchange and three pawns!. **18...Qxd6; 19.Kf2.** The result of the combination is a material advantage and continuing attack.

19...Qh6; 20.Bd4 Qh2+; 21.Ke1 Qxg3+; 22.Kd2 Qg2.

White could resign here. Black still has the initiative, as well as four extra pawns. **23.Nb2 Ba6; 24.Nd3 Bxd3; 25.Kxd3 Rbd8!** Black has not finished attacking. There will be no endgame. **26.Bf1 Qe4+; 27.Kc3 c5; 28.Bxc5 Qc6; 29.Kb3 Rb8+; 30.Ka3 Re5; 31.Bb4 Qb6. White resigned.**

194

(75) KARPOV - SALOV
Linares, 1993

Karpov's accomplishments at the legendary tournaments in Linares, Spain, are among his finest results. In this game, Karpov starts out with one of the slowest and quietest openings, and in the middlegame, launches a kingside attack which sets up a combination.

1.d4 Nf6; 2.c4 e6; 3.Nf3 b6; 4.g3. Karpov sticks to the traditional handling of the Queen's Indian. His arch-rival Kasparov elevated Petrosian's alternative 4.a3 or 4.Nc3, followed by 5.a3 to the main line. **4...Bb7; 5.Bg2 Be7; 6.Nc3 Ne4; 7.Bd2 Bf6; 8.0–0 0–0; 9.Rc1 c5; 10.d5 exd5; 11.cxd5 Nxd2; 12.Nxd2.**

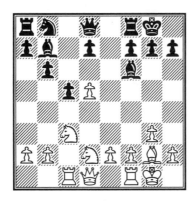

White has an advantage in space and the Black army is not positioned for effective defense. **12...d6; 13.Nde4 Be7; 14.f4.** This pawn is the spearhead of a pawn onslaught on the kingside. **14...Nd7; 15.g4 a6; 16.a4 Re8.** All this was well-known at the time, and Salov's new move is just a logical alternative to 16...Nf6. **17.g5 Bf8.**

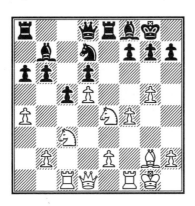

18.Kh1! Typical caution. Karpov will attack, but not at any risk to his own king, which is now safe. **18...b5; 19.axb5 axb5; 20.Nxb5 Qb6.** Now we see the logic behind Karpov's 18th move. There is no threatened discovered check.

21.Nbc3 Qb4; 22.Qd3 Nb6; 23.Qg3 Kh8; 24.Rcd1 Nc4; 25.b3 Nb6. Now a surprising move cracks open the Black position.

26.g6! fxg6. Taking with the other pawn also loses: 26...hxg6; 27.Qh4+ Kg8; 28.Ng5 and it is all over.

27.f5! gxf5; 28.Rxf5 Nd7; White's pieces quickly overwhelm the kingside. **29.Rdf1 Ne5; 30.R5f4 Qb6; 31.Ng5 Ng6.** Now for an elegant finish!

32.Nf7+ Kg8.

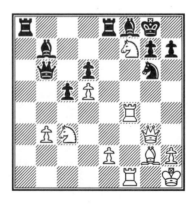

33.Qxg6!! The sacrifice of the queen forces checkmate on 33...hxg6; 34.Rh4 Be7; 35.Rh8#, so **Black resigned.**

(76) KARPOV - GEORGIEV
Tilburg, 1994

Even at the highest level of competition old themes resurface. Every beginner soon learns to protect the vulnerable f7 square as Black, not just in the opening, but throughout the game. Here Karpov shows, as White, that this topic is never far from his mind, though it takes some time before the weakness makes itself felt.

1.d4 Nf6; 2.c4 e6; 3.Nf3 d5; 4.Nc3 Be7; 5.Bg5 h6; 6.Bh4 0-0; 7.e3 b6; 8.Be2 Bb7; 9.Bxf6 Bxf6; 10.cxd5 exd5; 11.b4 c6.

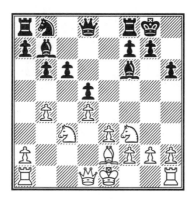

Black sometimes tries ...c5, which as been seen in quite a few Kasparov-Karpov contests. **12.0-0 Qd6.** There is no shortage of alternatives. 12...Re8 is considered acceptable, as are others.

13.Qb3 Nd7; 14.Rfe1 Be7. 14...Rfe8; 15.Bf1 Be7; 16.Rab1 a5; 17.bxa5 Rxa5; 18.a4 gave Karpov an advantage against Boensch, at Baden-Baden, 1992.

15.Rab1 a5; 16.bxa5 Rxa5; 17.a4 Re8; 18.Bf1 Bf8; 19.Qc2 g6.

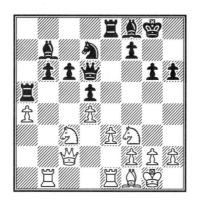

Karpov has a typical opening advantage. We can see that f7 is a bit neglected. There is no way to take advantage, however, while the game remains closed. Therefore, Karpov opens it up.

20.e4! dxe4; 21.Nxe4 Qf4; 22.Bc4 Bg7; 23.Re2 c5. Black struggles to find counterplay, but Karpov repels all efforts. **24.d5! Raa8; 25.Rbe1.** White is setting up tactical threats. Black now tries to reorganize to go after the pawn at d5. **25...Rad8; 26.Qb3 Ba8; 27.g3 Qb8; 28.d6!** Now the path to f7 is clear.

28...Rf8.

Black has defended the pawn, but Karpov has prepared a combination! **29.Bxf7+! Rxf7; 30.Neg5!!** All of White's pieces play their roles to perfection.

30...hxg5; 31.Nxg5 Rf8. Now, Karpov just blows down the walls and triumphantly enters the position. **32.Re8 Qxd6; 33.Qxf7+ Kh8; 34.Ne6. Black resigned.**

(77) KARPOV - COBO
Skopje Olympiad, 1972

Karpov shows that he is quite capable of breaking down barriers with sacrificial and combinative play in this next game.

1.e4 c5; 2.Nf3 d6; 3.d4 cxd4; 4.Nxd4 Nf6; 5.Nc3 a6; 6.f4 e6; 7.Be2 Qc7; 8.0-0 Nc6; 9.Kh1 Bd7; 10.a4 Be7; 11.Nb3 0-0; 12.Be3.

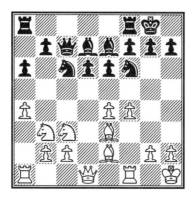

The opening is a typical Scheveningen Sicilian, and, in fact, this position is in keeping with all of the main ideas of that opening. So Black hasn't had to do much thinking yet. With the next move, Cobo makes an error in strategic judgement which turns out to be critical. The knight at c6 should head for c4 via a5, but instead goes to b4, in a vain attempt to carry out the Sicilian break with...d5.

12...Nb4?!; 13.a5 Bc6. 13...d5; 14.Bb6 Qc8; 15.e5 Ne4; 16.Nxe4 dxe4; 17.c4 leaves Black all tied down. **14.Bb6! Qb8?!** 14...Qd7; 15.Bf3 is better for White, but not as bad for Black as the text. **15.Qd2 d5.** Black has achieved the break, but under unfavorable circumstances, as the bishop at c6 is reduced to the status of an altar boy.

16.e5 Nd7. 16...Ne4; 17.Nxe4 dxe4; 18.c4 is also miserable for Black. **17.Bd4 b5; 18.Bg4 g6; 19.Rae1 Rc8; 20.f5 gxf5.** 20...exf5; 22.e6 opens up too many lines.

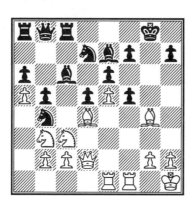

The kingside has no defense, and Karpov launches a combination which wins by force. **21.Bxf5.** If Black plays 21...exf5, then 22.e6 wins, according to Karpov. This requires a little more explanation.

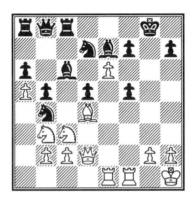

It is not merely that the knight on d7 is under attack. That, in fact, is irrelevant. Let's first dismiss 22...Nf6 on account of 23.Qg5+. 22...fxe6 is countered with 23.Rxe6. The retreat 22...Nf8 fails to the simple 23.exf7+ Kxf7; 24.Rxe7+ and mate in 6. So the knight can't be saved in any case. A reasonable plan is 22...Qd6; 23.Qh6 f6; 24.Rxf5 Nf8, but this leads to 25.Rg5+! Ng6; 26.Rxg6+! hxg6; 27.Qxg6+ Kh8; 28.Rd3 and 29.Rh3#.

Back to the game, where the action continues. **21...Nf8; 22.Qh6!**

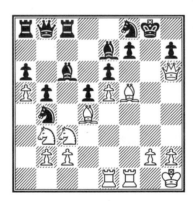

Before a successful combination can be launched, all pieces must be in position to reach useful squares. Here the White queen was not already on the kingside, but she sat on a square with direct access to crucial kingside dark squares. Karpov is not worried about the bishop at f5, as capturing it would allow White to blast open the e-file.

22...Ng6. Though Black declines the sacrifice, White's forcing variations continue. 22...exf5 allows 23.e6! and to avoid immediate disaster Black must play 23...f6. Now there follows 24.Rxf5 Nxc2 (24...Be8; 25.Rxf6) 25.Rg5+! The rook cannot be captured because of mate at g7, so there is nothing better than 25...Ng6; 26.Rxg6+! hxg6; 27.Qxg6+ Kh8; 28.Bxf6+ Bxf6; 29.Qxf6+ Kh7; 30.Re5 and mate follows.

23.Bxg6.

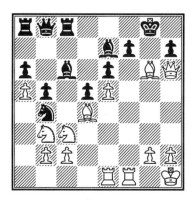

23...hxg6? Black could have put up stiffer resistance. 23...fxg6 forces White to find 24.Qh3! This excellent move keeps the pressure on. Black must now retreat the bishop to d7, but this takes away a valuable flight square. 24...Bd7; 25.Rf7. The threat of mate at h7 forces Black to accept this gift. 25...Kxf7; 26.Qxh7+ Ke8; 27.Qg8+ Bf8; 28.Rf1 Kd8; 29.Qxf8+ Be8. (29...Kc7; 30.Qd6+.) 30.Bb6+ Kd7. (30...Rc7; 31.Nc5.) 31.Rf7+ Bxf7; 32.Qxf7+ Kc6; 33.Nd4#.

24.Re3. Black must now cope with the threat of Rh3 and Qh8#. **24...Bf8; 25.Qh4 Bg7; 26.Rh3.** The combination has resulted in a winning position, because Black will not be able to cope with all the threats, the most deadly of them being Bc5 and Qh7#.

26...Be8; 27.Qh7+ Kf8; 28.Qxg6 f6.

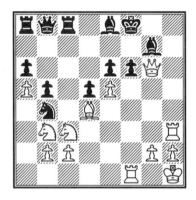

And a small sacrifice wraps things up. **29.Rxf6+. Black resigned.** 29...Bxf6; 30.Qxf6+ and 31.Rh8#.

(78) KARPOV - NUNN
Wijk Aan Zee, 1993

One would expect a sharp tactical brawl when Karpov plays against Nunn, and this game does not disappoint. Early in the game, it is superb tactician, John Nunn, offering a sacrifice. As the game goes on, we will see that it is Karpov who shows greater combinational insight, though his combination comes deep into a tactical endgame.

1.d4 Nf6; 2.c4 g6; 3.Nc3 Bg7; 4.e4 d6; 5.f3 0–0; 6.Be3 Nbd7; 7.Qd2 c5; 8.d5 Ne5; 9.Bg5 a6; 10.f4 Ned7; 11.Nf3 b5.

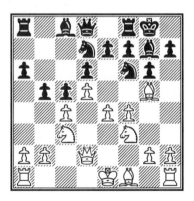

Right away Karpov is faced with a decision—to accept or decline? **12.cxb5.** 12.e5 b4; 13.Ne2 Ne4 would have given Black an active position, and the pressure on the pawn at e5 would be unbearable.

12...Qa5; 13.e5! Karpov grabs the initiative. **13...dxe5; 14.fxe5 Ng4; 15.Bxe7 Re8; 16.d6 Bh6.** The pawn at e5 is taboo. 16...Ndxe5; 17.Nxe5 Nxe5; 18.Nd5 Qxd2+; 19.Kxd2 is a tremendous endgame for White.

17.Ng5 Ngxe5; 18.Be2 axb5. 18...Rxe7; 19.dxe7 Bb7 would be plausible if Black could corral the e-pawn, but Karpov had planned 20.0–0! when Black does not have time for 20...Re8. After 20...f6; 21.Qd6! Bxg5. (21...fxg5; 22.Qe6+ Kg7 the pawn also advances to e8.) 22.Qe6+ Kg7; 23.bxa6 Be3+; 24.Kh1 Bxa6. The pawn promotes and Black must part with the rook. 25.e8Q Rxe8; 26.Qxe8 Bxe2; 27.Rfe1 and the e-file again proves decisive.

19.0–0 c4; 20.Bf3 Nxf3+; 21.Rxf3.

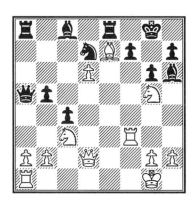

Black is already in serious trouble on the kingside and material is still even! **21...Ne5.** 21...Bb7 leads to 22.Rh3 Bxg5. (22...Bg7; 23.Rxh7 Qb6+; 24.Kh1 f6; 25.Rxg7+!! Kxg7; 26.Ne6+ Kh7.) 23.Qxg5 Qb6+; 24.Kh1. **22.Re3.** 22.Qd5 Nxf3+; 23.gxf3 Bxg5; 24.Qxg5 Qb6+; 25.Kg2 Bf5; 26.Nd5 Qd4; 27.Nf6+ Kh8; 28.Nxe8 Qxb2+; 29.Kg3 Qe5+ is just a draw! **22...Nd3; 23.Rf1.** White might have tried 23.b4 here instead.

23...Be6; 24.h4 Bf8.

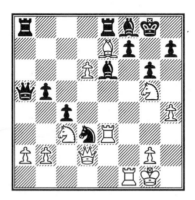

Nunn strikes again, sacrificing a pawn at e6 to draw the pawn at d6 to a more vulnerable square. Perhaps Karpov should have just exchanged bishops at f8.

25.Nxe6 fxe6; 26.Rxe6 b4! Black drives Karpov's knight back to a pathetic square before swapping bishops at e7. **27.Nd1.** 27.Ne4 looks better, but it isn't. 27...Bxe7; 28.dxe7 Qa7+; 29.Kh2 Rxe7 and now 30.Nf6+ Kg7 leaves White facing difficulties, with a weak pawn at a2, unresolved rook at e6, and menacing Black forces on the queenside. Yet there is more than meets the eye here. White can continue the attack by a combination.

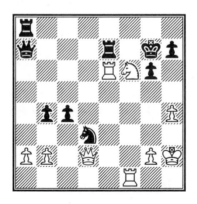

31.Nh5+! is critical. Black must not play 31...Kg8; 32.Qe2! Qc7+; 33.g3 Ra7. (33...Rxe6; 34.Qxe6+ Kh8; 35.Rf7 and Black must part with the queen.) 34.Qe4!! gxh5; 35.Qd5! Rxe6; 36.Qxe6+ Qf7. (36...Kh8; 37.Rf8+ Kg7; 38.Qf6#.) 37.Rxf7 Rxf7; 38.Qxc4 Ne5;

39.Qxb4 Ng4+; 40.Kg2 Rf2+; 41.Kg1 and Black can resign, as the a-pawn will race up the board after Black deals with the immediate threat of 42.Qxg4+ followed by Kxf2.

More accurate is 31...Kh8!, which forces White to take radical measures, as too much material is hanging and, in any case, Black threatens to consolidate with ...Rg8. 32.Rxg6! is the best reply. 32...hxg6; 33.Qh6+ Kg8; 34.Qxg6+ Kh8. (34...Rg7; 35.Nxg7 Qxg7; 36.Qe6+ Kh8; 37.Rf6! and White wins the Black queen for the rook.) 35.Qh6+ Kg8; 36.Nf6+ Kf7; 37.Qh5+! Kf8; 38.Nd5+ Kg8. (38...Nf2; 39.Qh8+ Kf7; 40.Qf6+ picks off the knight.) 39.Nf6+ Kf8. This long forced variation leads to the following position.

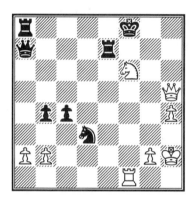

As a result of the combination (so far) White has cracked open the Black kingside. However, with only two pawns for a rook, White must find some way to continue the forcing nature of the position. Simply winning the rook at e7 for the knight would leave White with only two pawns for the piece, and the queenside pawns are both under attack. 40.Nd5+ Kg8; 41.Nxe7+ Qxe7. With superb maneuvering, White is now ready to pose an unanswerable question to Black. 42.Rf3! (42.Qd5+ Kg7; 43.Qxa8 Qxh4+; 44.Kg1 Qd4+ and Black escapes with a draw.) 42...Qe5+; 43.Rg3+!

White maintains the initiative even in defense. Glorious! Black can give up the queen now, but would have no chance in the endgame. 43...Kf8; 44.Qf3+ Qf4; 45.Qxa8+ Ke7; 46.Qh8. White defends the weak pawns at b2 and h4 and can convert the material advantage. One can argue that this entire line is a huge combination, but it is highly unlikely that Karpov, or any human, could calculate it. In fact, we performed this analysis with the assistance from powerful computers, which could not come close to finding the main line.

Back to the game!

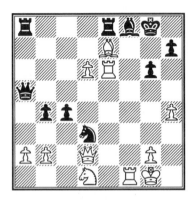

27...Bxe7; 28.Qe3 Qc5. 28...Qa7; 29.Rxe7 Qxe3+; 30.Nxe3 Rxe7; 31.dxe7 Re8; 32.Nxc4 Rxe7; 33.Rd1 Re4; 34.b3 is a superior endgame for White.

29.dxe7 Rxa2; 30.Kh1 Ra7.

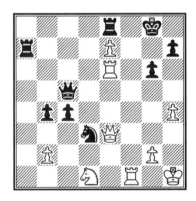

While the goal of involving all forces in the attack is an admirable one, sometimes it is just not possible. The knight at d1 just can't get involved. Therefore, White is limited to attacking with a queen and two rooks, with an assist from the pawn at e7. Given that the Black king has only two small pawns as defenders, it is more than enough to justify a sacrifice. Besides, White's position is awful, despite the pawn at e7. Black is cruising down the queenside and the e-pawn is not going anywhere except, perhaps, back into the box.

31.Rxg6+!? hxg6; 32.Qe6+ Kg7; 33.Qf7+ Kh6; 34.Qxe8.

Karpov has recovered the material, and is a pawn ahead. More important than the pawn, however, is the vulnerable position of the enemy king. Although the forcing variation seems to have come to an end, that is not the case.

The combination continues, as Black is still forced to deal with immediate threats. In the present position, White threatens not only Qh8#, but also Qf8+, followed by the advance of the pawn to e8.

34...Qxe7. 34...Rxe7 is much stronger. 35.Qh8+ Rh7; 36.Qd8 seems to be the best White can do, and with equal material, White's positional advantage and the vulnerable targets on the queenside are offset by the insecure position of his own king. So what we have seen so far, is a sacrifice, but not a combination, unless one can argue for a significant advantage for White here. 36...Qe7; 37.Qd4 Qc5 and Black should have no problem drawing. **35.Qh8+ Qh7; 36.Qd4.** Now the threat is the capture of the pawn at c4 and the Black knight is ready to fall. **36...Qe7; 37.Ne3 Ne5.**

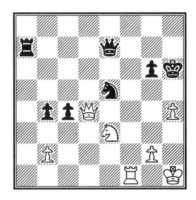

If the previous sacrifice fails to qualify as a combination, Karpov makes a clear combinative statement with his next move. 37...c3 loses to 38.Qh8+ Qh7; 39.Ng4+ Kh5; 40.Nf6+.

38.Qxe5! Qxh4+. 38...Qxe5; 39.Ng4+ Kg7; 40.Nxe5 c3; 41.bxc3 bxc3; 42.Rc1 is a simple win for White. **39.Kg1 Re7; 40.Qh8+ Rh7; 41.Qf8+ Rg7.** Karpov probably repeated the position in order to insure that he made time control. **42.Qh8+ Rh7; 43.Qf8+ Rg7; 44.Rf3! Black resigned.**

FIND THE WIN!

(49) KARPOV - ALBURT
Malta Olympiad, 1980

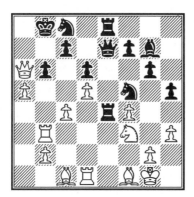

The light squares provide all the illumination needed for victory.

(50) KARPOV - OFIESH
Simultaneous Exhibition, 1991

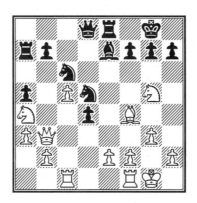

(51) KARPOV - CSOM
Bad Lauterberg, 1977

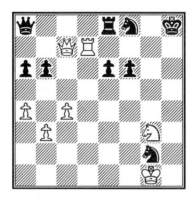

Both kings are naked but for a single defensive knight. White must hurry, however.

(52) TARJAN - KARPOV
Skopje, 1976

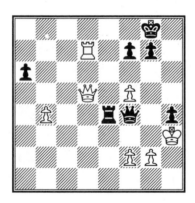

How can Black finish off the game?

16. GARRY KASPAROV

Thirteenth World Champion
(FIDE 1985–1993, PCA 1993–Present)

Kasparov is considered, by many, to be the greatest chessplayer of all time. In *Warriors of the Mind*, mathematician Nathan Divinsky and co-author Keene studied the results of all the great players and calculated rankings, with Kasparov firmly at the top. In this book, we are concerned exclusively with the art of the combination, and here too it can be argued that Kasparov is without equal.

Kasparov has a very aggressive style, and is often willing to invest material for an attack or other positional compensation. Unlike Tal, his attacks are not mostly aimed at the enemy king. Instead, Kasparov fights hard, perhaps without parallel, to seize the initiative. Then he will target weaknesses in the enemy position, wherever they can be found. After tying down the enemy forces to the defense of the weak area, Kasparov then launches the attack against the enemy king.

The feisty nature of Kasparov's personality, exhibited on and off the chessboard, makes him a relentless opponent. He is constantly looking for combinations, and produces them in almost every tournament and World Championship match. He can even use them against a computer, while playing blindfold, as we will see. The brilliant moves used to conquer human opponents are at least as impressive!

(79) KASPAROV - GAVRIKOV
Soviet Championship, 1981

Our first game illustrates Kasparov's ability to apply pressure on a portion of the board, far from the enemy king, in order to bring about the preconditions for a successful attack. Combinations are a part of Kasparov's arsenal, usually used in the decisive final assault, as follows.

1.d4 d5; 2.c4 e6; 3.Nf3 c5; 4.cxd5 exd5; 5.g3 Nc6; 6.Bg2 Nf6; 7.0–0 Be7; 8.dxc5 Bxc5; 9.Bg5 0–0; 10.Nc3 d4; 11.Bxf6 Qxf6; 12.Nd5 Qd8; 13.Nd2.

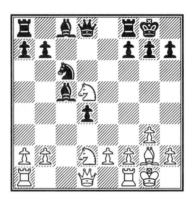

This is the one of the main lines of the Tarrasch Defense, and at the time there were three moves which were considered playable for Black: ...Bg4, ...Re8, and ...a6. This game eliminated the last from serious competition, in spectacular fashion!

13...a6; 14.Rc1 Ba7; 15.Nc4 Rb8. This is artificial, and Black should have developed the light-squared bishop.

16.Nf4 b5? A critical error by Gavrikov, who was reeling from the strength of Kasparov's opening play. White now uses a small combinational flurry, based on the weakness of the knight at c6, to achieve a strong position.

17.Nd6! Qxd6; 18.Rxc6 Qd8; 19.Qc2 a5; 20.Rc1 Re8; 21.Bd5.

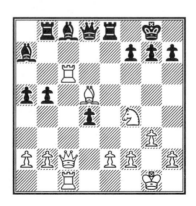

White's pieces dominate the board, but don't seem to be targeting the kingside. Actually, the move Kasparov played is part of a long and amazing journey. The light squares belong to this bishop, who will use them to great effect.

21...Bb6. Black's position is falling apart, so counterplay with 21...d3 was indicated. **22.Qb3.** A simple fork of pawns at b5 and f7. **22...Re7; 23.Bf3!** 23.Qxb5? Bd7 gives White compensation for the exchange, but no more. **23...Re5; 24.Bh5!** The bishop, tired from its long journey, prepares to make the ultimate sacrifice. **24...g6.**

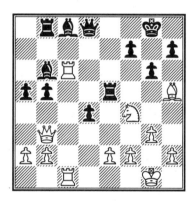

25.Bxg6!! hxg; 26.Rxg6+. The pin on the pawn at f7 is now revealed to be the true reason behind Kasparov's 22nd move.

26...Kf8; 27.Rh6 Ke7. 27...Kg7 sets up another brilliant finish.

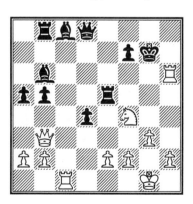

28.Rh7+!! Kxh7; 29.Qxf7+ Kh8; 30.Ng6#. In the game, we see a different theme. **28.Rcc6!** The threat is Ng6+! Kasparov creates a fence along the 6th rank, keeping the Black king completely contained.

28...Rf5; 29.Qf3 Bc7; 30.Qe4+ Re5.

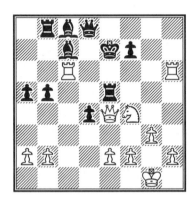

Black is hanging on, but another combination brings the Black monarch to his knees in submission. **31.Ng6+!! fxg6; 32.Rh7+ Kf8; 33.Qxg6. Black resigned.**

(80) KASPAROV - YUSUPOV
Soviet Championship, 1981

Kasparov's ability to find a way through the defensive barrier characterized his ascent to the World Championship. This game contains one of the most impressive of all of Kasparov's combinations. Kasparov blasts open a seemingly blocked position in the manner of some mean and particularly ravenous dinosaur. The Black king is accessible only via an open file, which Black can easily control.

1.d4 Nf6; 2.c4 e6; 3.Nf3 Bb4+; 4.Bd2 a5; 5.g3 0–0; 6.Bg2 b6; 7.0–0 Ba6; 8.Bg5 Be7; 9.Qc2 Nc6; 10.a3 h6; 11.Bxf6 Bxf6; 12.Rd1 Qe7; 13.e3 Rae8?!

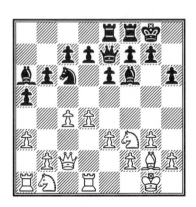

In this slow opening, Black has actually outstripped White's development, but that is only an illusory advantage. White controls the center, and d7-d5 will not be appropriate because of the position of the White queen, putting pressure on the c-file.

14.Nfd2 g5?! Black overreacts to the positional strength of White's game. 14...g6 would have been more solid. **15.Nc3 Bg7; 16.Nb5 Qd8; 17.f4 Ne7!** Black has taken advantage of White's faulty plan by reorganizing his pieces so that the Ne7 can take part in the defense. Unfortunately, Yusupov soon forgets why he wanted the knight at e7.

18.Nf3 Nf5; 19.Qf2 c6; 20.Nc3 gxf4; 21.gxf4 Bxc4. The pawn at c4 would have helped White to break through at d5, but Kasparov has eyes only for the kingside. **22.e4 Nd6?** 22...Ne7; 23.Kh1! f5; 24.e5 brings White sufficient compensation for his pawn, because Black's kingside is very weak.

23.Ne5 f5; 24.Nxc4 Nxc4; 25.b3! The Black knight is driven back to its home rank. **25...Nd6; 26.e5 Nc8; 27.Bf3 Kh7; 28.Bh5 Re7; 29.Kh1 Rg8?!** 29...Bh8; 30.Rg1 Rg7; 31.Rxg7+ Bxg7; 32.Rg1 Qe7! would have been relatively best.

30.Rg1 Bh8.

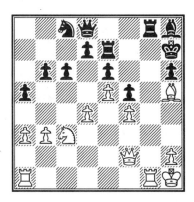

The Black king is suffocating at h7, but there does not seem to be any way to attack it. Black threatens to use the g-file to exchange the heavy pieces, and in an endgame White may suffer because of the weaknesses of the pawn structure. Kasparov's solution is ingenious and original, but makes use of the same themes seen in thousands of other combinations.

31.Ne4!! The combination begins with the offer of the knight, which must be accepted because of the threat of Nf6+. This gives White access to the f5-square. The sacrifice of material is not of great importance because Black's knight is so out of play.

31...fxe4; 32.f5 Rg5? Bringing the queen to f8 would have been better (Black cannot play 32...Reg7 because of 33.Bg6+). 32...Qf8. White now does not check with the bishop, as Black would sacrifice the rook for it, but instead advances 33.f6! Black's most ingenious defense is 33...Reg7, exploiting the pin on the f-file. After 34.Rxg7 Bxg7 there is the resource 35.f7!

It doesn't matter much what Black plays here, since White will have a serious advantage after capturing the rook with check. If 35...Rh8; 36.Qg2 Ne7; 37.Qxe4+ Nf5; 38.Qg1 Black has nothing better than 38...Rg8 and then White easily wins the endgame after 39.fxg8+.

33.Rxg5 hxg5; 34.f6.

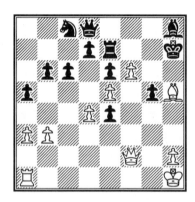

34...Kh6. This is pretty much forced. 34...Qf8; 35.fxe7 Qxf2; 36.e8Q wins because Black has no checks. **35.fxe7 Qxe7.** 35...Nxe7 doesn't help. 36.Qf7 Bg7; 37.Rf1 Bh8; 38.Rf6+ Bxf6; 39.exf6 and **White wins. 36.Bf7! d6.** 36...g4 is refuted by 37.h4! gxh3; 38.Rg1 Bg7; 39.Qf4+ Kh7; 40.Qxe4+ Kh8; 41.Qg6.

37.Rf1 g4.

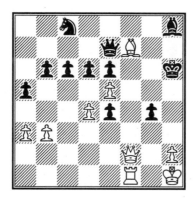

A final, elegant, combinative touch brings the game to an end. 37...dxe5 would have led to death on the dark squares after 38.Qe2. **38.Bxe6!! Qxe6; 39.Qh4+ Kg7** and here Yusupov resigned before Kasparov could play 40.Rf6. **1–0.**

(81) KASPAROV - ANAND
PCA World Championship, 1995

Combinations are generally invented at the chessboard, but sometimes, as we have seen, they are part of careful home preparation. This game is perhaps the most spectacular example of a prepared combination, and its significance is enhanced by the fact that it was unveiled in a critical game of the 1995 World Championship. Kasparov refined an idea suggested by World Champion Mikhail Tal, so this is truly a World Champion combination!

1.e4 e5; 2.Nf3 Nc6; 3.Bb5 a6; 4.Ba4 Nf6; 5.0–0 Nxe4; 6.d4 b5; 7.Bb3 d5; 8.dxe5 Be6; 9.Nbd2. This move has moved up to an equal position with 9.c3 as the main line of the Open Spanish.

9...Nc5; 10.c3 d4. Anand takes up the challenge of the aggressive main line.

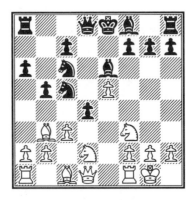

11.Ng5. This introduces a piece sacrifice which leads to unclear complications if accepted. Anand had prepared an alternative line. **11...dxc3.** 11...Qxg5; 12.Qf3 0-0-0; 13.Bxe6+ fxe6; 14.Qxc6 is a well-explored alternative for Black.

12.Nxe6 fxe6; 13.bxc3 Qd3. This much had been seen in game #6 of the match, but in this game Kasparov was ready with an old new move from the magical hand of Mikhail Tal.

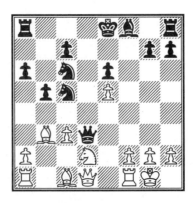

14.Bc2!! Tal's idea is to set up a magnificent rook sacrifice. Kasparov claimed that the idea had only come to his attention a few days before this game. In any case, Kasparov had the luxury of exploring the wild complications in the comfort of his home, and was able to work out all the details and check them with powerful computers.

14...Qxc3. Anand responded quickly and seemed to be well within his own preparation. **15.Nb3 Nxb3.** Amazingly, even this much is not new. An obscure postal game between Berg and Nevestveit in 1990 reached the same position, and varied with 15...Rd8. After, 16.Bd2 Qxc5, Kasparov would have revealed the strong original move 17.Qg4! Better is 16...Rxd2!; 17.Nxd2 and then a capture at e5. **16.Bxb3 Nd4.** Anand defers acceptance of the sacrifice until the next move. After 16...Qxa1; 17.Qh5+, it is hard to find a defense for Black.

    17.Qg4 Qxa1; 18.Bxe6.

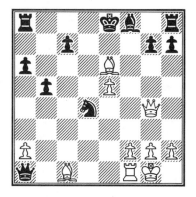

    Black has an extra rook, but the king, trapped in the center, will pay a high price. **18...Rd8.** 18...Nxe6; 19.Qxe6+ Be7; 20.Bg5 is immediately terminal. **19.Bh6 Qc3.** Not 19...Qxf1+?; 20.Kxf1 gxh6; 21.Qh5+.

    20.Bxg7 Qd3; 21.Bxh8 Qg6. 21...Ne2+ only postpones the inevitable. **22.Bf6 Be7; 23.Bxe7 Qxg4.** Or 23...Kxe7; 24.Qh4+. **24.Bxg4 Kxe7; 25.Rc1.** No longer in home preparation, Kasparov needs no assistance to win this endgame.

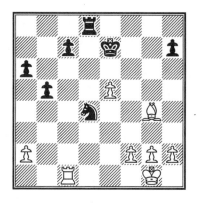

25...c6; 26.f4 a5; 27.Kf2 a4; 28.Ke3 b4; 29.Bd1. The bishop gets out of the way so that the g-pawn can advance. **29...a3; 30.g4 Rd5; 31.Rc4 c5; 32.Ke4 Rd8; 33.Rxc5 Ne6; 34.Rd5 Rc8; 35.f5 Rc4+; 36.Ke3 Nc5; 37.g5 Rc1; 38.Rd6. Black resigned**

(82) KASPAROV - MEPHISTO (COMPUTER)
Blindfold Simultaneous, 1985

Kasparov played the following game in a simultaneous exhibition, where he faced a total of ten opponents, and had just 90 minutes to make 40 moves against each of them. That is quite a handicap! Now consider that one of his opponents was a powerful computer. Usually combinations are sidestepped by computers, but here Kasparov creates an avalanche of combinative blows. The machine has a devil of a time defending, and eventually has to capitulate.

1.e4 e5; 2.Nf3 Nc6; 3.Bb5 a6; 4.Ba4 Nf6; 5.0-0 Be7; 6.Re1 b5; 7.Bb3 d6; 8.c3 0-0; 9.h3 Na5; 10.Bc2 c5; 11.d4 Qc7; 12.d5 Bd7; 13.b3 Qb6.

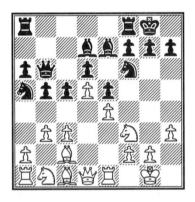

Black's passive play leaves him without a plan. The formations with ...Bd7 are not considered very good these days. Kasparov lost to Deeper Blue in their 1997 match from a related structure as Black. **14.Nbd2 Rfc8; 15.Nf1.** White adopts the century-old plan of shifting the knight to the kingside where it can leap to f5.

15...h6; 16.Be3 Qd8; 17.Qd2 Nh7; 18.Ng3 Rab8; 19.Nf5! Bxf5; 20.exf5 Nf6; 21.g4.

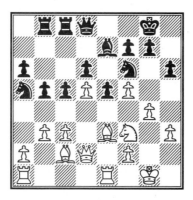

Black has no counterplay at all, and White is free to slowly build up in preparation for a decisive combination. **21...Nh7; 22.Kg2 Rb7; 23.Rh1 Nf6; 24.Rag1 Qb6; 25.Kf1 Rd7.** A typical Kasparov combination is just a few steps away. The sight of all those Black pieces on squares far from their monarch must have had Garry drooling.

26.g5 hxg5; 27.Nxg5 Qb7.

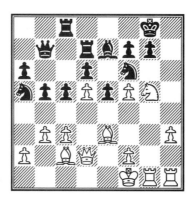

Now Kasparov must pick up the pace, since the pawn at d5 is ready to fall and there is only one open line to the enemy king. Many players would calculate a sacrifice at f7 here, but it is g7 that is the target. Kasparov starts the forced variation by attacking it twice.

28.Ne6!! fxe6; 29.fxe6 Rdc7.

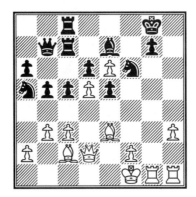

Kasparov is properly obsessed with g7, and continues to hack away at it. **30.Rxg7+!! Kxg7; 31.Bh6+ Kh8.** Not to belabor the point, but g7 beckons. **32.Bg7+!** This final sacrifice forces mate. **32...Kxg7. 32...Kg8; 33.Qh6. 33.Qg5+ Kf8; 34.Qh6+ Ke8; 35.Bg6+ Kd8; 36.Qh8+. Black resigned.**

(83) KASPAROV - SEIRAWAN
Amsterdam, 1996

Because the modern professional is a better defender than in the past, we find more and more combinations buried in side-variations to the game. The defense is better able to spot the combinations in advance, and they are therefore less likely to see the light of the chessboard until the post-mortem.

1.d4 Nf6; 2.c4 e6; 3.Nf3 d5; 4.Nc3 Nbd7; 5.Qc2. An uncommon move which throws Black on his own resources. Instead, 5.Bg5 c6; 6.e3 Qa5 would transpose to the well-worn paths of the Cambridge Springs variation.

5...dxc4. In view of what happens, this surrender of the center for temporary material gains may be too risky. 5...c6 is a solid alternative.

6.e4 c5; 7.dxc5 Bxc5; 8.Bxc4 a6; 9.a4 Qc7; 10.0–0.

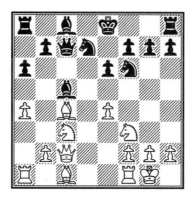

10...Ng4. Black could already go for the immediate win of a pawn with 10...Bxf2+; 11.Qxf2; Qxc4, 12.e5 Ng4; 13.Qg3 or 12...Nd5, when again 13.Qg3 gives White a strong attack. With the move of the text, Seirawan hopes to win more than a pawn and to remove White's dangerous king's rook in the process. **11.h3 Nxf2.** Black could have equalized with 11...Nge5. **12.Rxf2 Bxf2+; 13.Qxf2 Qxc4; 14.Qg3 f6.**

A sudden reversal of his previous policy of unrestrained gluttony, but if 14...g6 then 15.Bh6, leaves Black's king pinned down in the center, while 14...0–0; 15. Bh6 g6; 16. Rd1 gives White a terrible attack with moves such as Qh4 or Ng5 in the offing.

15.Qxg7 Qc5+; 16.Kh1 Qf8; 17.Qg4 Qf7.

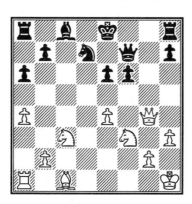

Black is a clear exchange, i.e. rook for knight, ahead, but his forces remain largely dormant and he cannot castle. Such a position is meat and drink to Kasparov. **18.e5!** Offering a further pawn to prepare the murderous incursion Ne4, Black hastens to deny White the use of this square. A Morphy opponent would probably have played 18...Nxe5; 19.Nxe5 fxe5; 20.Ne4 Qf1+; 21.Kh2 Kf7; 22.Bh6 Qxa1; 23.Qg7+ Ke8; 24.Bg5 and Black is mated as a result of the combination. After 21...Rf8, White wins with 22.Qg7 Qd3; 23.Bh6! In declining the material, Black allows White to maintain the initiative. Although the win lies far in the future, the result of the strong advance of the e-pawn is felt for some time.

18...Rg8; 19.Qc4 f5; 20.Bg5 h6; 21.Bh4 Qg6. Briefly threatening mate himself, but Black has little chance of developing a genuine attack. **22.Rg1 Nf8; 23.Qb4 Rg7; 24.Ne2.**

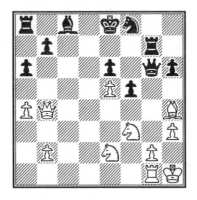

24...b5. Violent measures to burst free from his straitjacket. Failing this, White simply tightens the noose with moves such as Nf4 and Rd1. **25.axb5** Kasparov had a win here with 25.Nc4! Qf7; 26.Bf6 Rg8; 27.axb5 and a crush. **25...Rd7; 26.Nf4.** Forcing the black queen back from its active post. **26...Qf7; 27.Rc1 Bb7; 28.bxa6 Bxf3.** The bishop's career is brief. With this exchange, Black speculates that the fracturing of the pawn structure around White's king may give him some prospects of a perpetual check. **29.gxf3 Rda7; 30.Rg1.** As Black nears emancipation on the queen's flank, Kasparov switched fronts. The g-file, which had once been Black's territory, is now to be used as a focal point for the white invasion.

30...Rxa6; 31.Nh5 Qc7. Of course not. 31...Qxh5 on account of 32.Qe7 **checkmate. 32.Rg7 Ra1+; 33.Kg2 Qc2+; 34.Bf2.** Having escaped the checks from Black's brief outburst of activity, White's attacking formation is now complete. In order to prevent checkmate at e7, Black must play 34...Ra1–a7. However, disaster strikes from a different direction, namely 35.Nf6+ Kd8; 36.Qxf8 mate. A remarkable feature of this game is that Black lost, without castling, and without having once moved his queen's rook.

(84) KASPAROV - NIKOLIC
Linares, 1997

Our final example is another game in which the brilliant combinations are partially submerged, because Nikolic is too sophisticated a defender to fall for the prettiest of the tactics. This is typical of Kasparov's ability to construct such complex combinations that even when the defender has a path to defend against immediate threats, the pressure is still strong enough to force victory.

The result of the combination is not necessarily an immediate checkmate or win of material, but rather a situation which is so favorable that even the best defense by the opponent must inevitably fail. The sacrifice, an essential part of the combination, is often declined, but the power of the move is in no way diminished.

1.e4 e5; 2.Nf3 Nc6; 3.d4. The opening has been one of Kasparov's favorites, the Scotch, first introduced in a correspondence match between Edinburgh and London in 1824. Interestingly, it was the London club that first tried the variation, but the honor of acquiring the name strangely went to Edinburgh!

3...exd4; 4.Nxd4 Nf6; 5.Nxc6 bxc6; 6.e5 Qe7; 7.Qe2 Nd5; 8.c4 Ba6; 9.b3 g5. An amazing idea, played by Anand with reasonable success against Kasparov in their 1995 World Championship match. The move looks insane, since it wrecks Black's kingside pawns. However, after 10.Ba3 d6; 11.exd6 Qxe2+; 12 Bxe2 Bg7, as played by Kasparov in the stem game, White could prove nothing. Here, Kasparov comes prepared. **10.g3 Bg7; 11.Bb2 0-0; 12.Nd2 f6.**

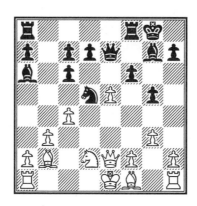

13.Qh5. Kasparov immediately gets to the heart of the matter. Black's ...g5 has weakened squares and pawns in the vicinity of his king. That is where Kasparov concentrates his army. **13...Nb4; 14.h4.** A fascinating combinational situation. If now 14...Nc2+; 15.Kd1 Nxa1; 16.hxg5 with multiple threats against Black's king.

14...g4.

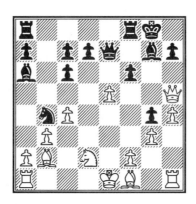

Thwarting White's intention to open the h-file, but now Kasparov comes up with a serious threat in another quarter. **15.Kd1.** We have arrived at the culmination of the operation that allowed Black to fork White's king and rook, and this culmination, by a forced tactical sequence, now wins material for White. Black is now threatened with a3, trapping his knight. Once it retreats, White will follow up with Bd3 and Re1, effectively mobilizing the rest of his forces.

15...c5; 16.a3 Nc6; 17.Bd3 f5; 18.Bxf5 Bxe5; 19.Re1. All has gone according to plan, and White now wins material by force. **19...d6; 20.Be4 Bb7; 21.Qxg4+ Qg7.** Tantamount to resignation, but if 21...Kh8; 22.Bxc6 Bxc6; 23.f4 and White wins a piece.

22.Bd5+ Kh8; 23.Bxe5 dxe5; 24.Qxg7+ Kxg7; 25.Ne4 Rad8; 26.Nxc5 Bc8; 27.Ra2. Apart from being two pawns down, Black is also unable, in the long run, to salvage his pawn on e5. One of Kasparov's most original and best games.

FIND THE WIN!

(53) KASPAROV - BROWNE
Banja Luka, 1979

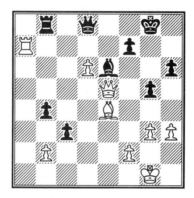

White's pieces do not seem to be attacking the enemy king, but the key to this position is a sacrifice followed by a pin.

(54) KASPAROV - MARTINOVIC
Baku, 1980

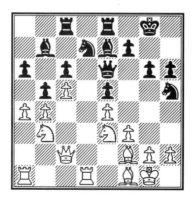

White to move. Concentrate on the queenside and infiltrate!

(55) KASPAROV - KARPOV
WORLD CHAMPIONSHIP, 1985

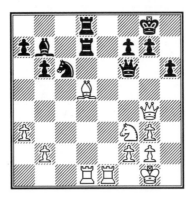

Even in a World Championship simple combinations can be overlooked. What did Karpov miss?

(56) KASPAROV - LARSO
EXHIBITION INTERNET, 1995

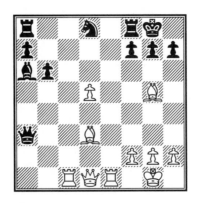

In our final task, White's starting move is perhaps obvious. Make sure you work out all of the details!

17. ANSWERS TO THE PROBLEMS

(1) DE RIVIERE - MORPHY
Paris, 1863

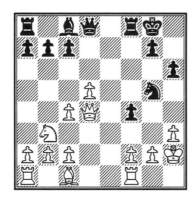

1...Nf3+!? Is this a combination or a sacrifice? As we have seen, Morphy's play was more sacrificial than combinational, and in this case the sacrifice does not lead, directly, to a checkmate. It does, however, produce a winning position. **2.gxf3 Qh4; 3.Rh1.** 3.Nd2 Bxh3; 4.Ne4 Bg4+; 5.Kg2 Qh3+; 6.Kg1 Bxf3 and there is nothing to be done about mate at g2. **3...Bxh3.** 3...Qxh3+; 4.Kg1 would not have accomplished anything.

4.Bd2. This was just a waste of time. 4.Bxf4 Rxf4; 5.Qe3 is critical, and the question here is whether Morphy had found any clear win. 5...Rf5! does the trick. **4...Rf6. White resigned.**

5.Bxf4 Rxf4; 6.Qe3. 6.Qxf4 Qxf4+; 7.Kxh3 Qxf3+; 8.Kh2 Qxf2+; 9.Kh3 Rf8 and mate in 4. **6...Rf5** is the same win as in the note to move 4.

(2) MARACHE - MORPHY
USA, 1857

Watch the knights dance: **1...Ng3!!; 2.Qxg6 Nde2#.**

(3) MORPHY - DE RIVIERE
Paris, 1858

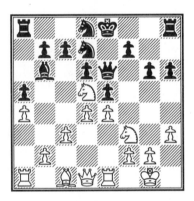

A sacrifice at h6 does the trick. **1.Bxh6! Rxh6; 2.Ng5.**

(4) MORPHY - MONGREDIEN
Paris, 1859

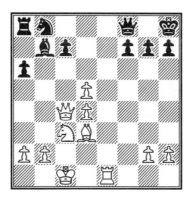

1.Qb4! Qc8; 2.Qxb7! **Black resigned** because of 2...Qxb7; 3.Re8#.

(5) STEINITZ - SCOTT
Dundee, 1867

The key here is the pin on the d-file and a8-f8 diagonal. **1.c4! Bxc4; 2.Qxd6 Rxd6; 3.Bxc5 Re6; 4.Rxe6 fxe6; 5.Bxf8 Kxf8; 6.Rc1 Bd5; 7.Rc8+. Black resigned.**

(6) STEINITZ - BLACKBURNE
London, 1876

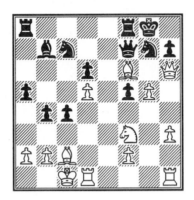

1.g6! Qxg6. 1...Qxf6; 2.Qxh7#, 1...hxg6; 2.Ng5! and the threat of Qh7# wins. **2.Bxg7 Qxh6+.** If 2...Qxg7; 3.Rhg1 wins. **3.Bxh6,** and White has an extra piece.

(7) STEINITZ - CHIGORIN
World Championship, Match Havana, 1892

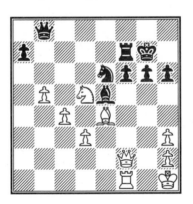

1.Bxg6! Kxg6; 2.Qf5+ Kg7; 3.Qxe6. White hasn't merely won a pawn, he has also cracked open the enemy shell and the enemy king is exposed. **3...Qb7; 4.d4 Bb8; 5.Rg1+ Kf8; 6.Qf5 Bd6; 7.c5 Be7; 8.c6. Black resigned.**

(8) REINER - STEINITZ
Vienna, 1860

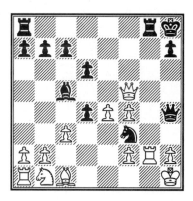

The g1 square beckons. **1...Qxh2+; 2.Rxh2 Rg1#.**

(9) LASKER - STEINITZ,
World Championship (2nd game), 1896

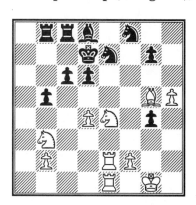

Lasker broke through with **1.Nec5+ dxc5; 2.Nxc5+ Kd6?** This gets mated, but 2...Kc7; 3.Bxe7 was not worth playing. **3.Bf4+ Kd5; 4.Re5+ Kc4; 5.Rc1+ Kxd4; 6.Re4+ Kd5; 7.Rd1+ Kxc5; 8.Be3#.**

(10) JANOWSKI - LASKER
Paris, 1909

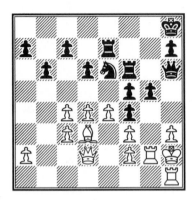

1...g4!; 2.Be2. 2.fxg4 Ng5 threatens the deadly ...Nf3#. 3.Qd1 Qxh3+; 4.Kg1 Nf3+ is also terminal. Or 2.exf5 Ng5! when h3 and f3 are indefensible. **2...Ng5!; 3.fxg4 f3; 4.Rg3 fxe2.**

(11) LASKER - PIRC
Moscow, 1935

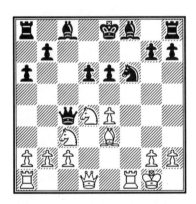

This is a long combination, but the play is forced. **1.Rxf6! gxf6; 2.Qh5+ Kd8.** 2...Kd7; 3.Qf7+ Be7; 4.Nf5 Re8; 5.Rd1 wins for White, as does 2...Ke7; 3.Nf5+! exf5; 4.Nd5+ Kd8; 5.Bb6++- Kd7; 6.Qf7+ Kc6; 7.Qc7+ Kb5; 8.a4+ Qxa4; 9.Nc3+ Kb4; 10.Rxa4#. **3.Qf7 Bd7.** Different checkmates greet the development of the other bishop. 3...Be7; 4.Nf5 Re8. (4...Qc7; 5.Na4 Rf8; 6.Qxh7 Ke8; 7.Bb6! Qd7; 8.Qh5+ Rf7; 9.Ng7+ Kf8; 10.Qh8#.) 5.Nxd6 Bxd6; 6.Bb6+ Bc7;

7.Rd1+ Qd5; 8.Bxc7#. **4.Qxf6+ Kc7; 5.Qxh8 Bh6; 6.Nxe6+! Qxe6; 7.Qxa8 Bxe3+; 8.Kh1.**

(12) LASKER - FORBES-ROBERTSON
Cheltenham, 1898

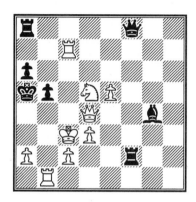

The win is achieved by removing Black's a-pawn.**1.Rxb5+!! axb5,** or 1...Kxb5; 2.Qb6+ Ka4; 3.Rc4+ Ka3; 4.Qb3+, **2.Qa7+!! Rxa7; 3.Rxa7#.**

(13) CAPABLANCA - FONAROFF
New York, 1904

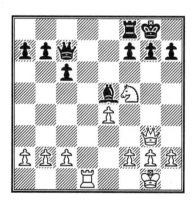

Black's position falls apart after **1.Nh6+ Kh8; 2.Qxe5! Qxe5; 3.Nxf7+!**

(14) CAPABLANCA - MIESES
Berlin, 1931

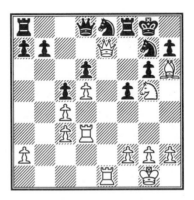

The drama takes place on the back rank. **1.Qxf8+! Kxf8; 2.Ne6+ Kf7; 3.Nxd8+. Black resigned.**

(15) CAPABLANCA - YATES
Barcelona, 1929

The White pawn promotes to deflect the enemy queen. **1.Rc7+ Bd7; 2.f8Q+ Qxf8; 3.Rxd7+.**

(16) CAPABLANCA - LASKER
Berlin Speed Game, 1914

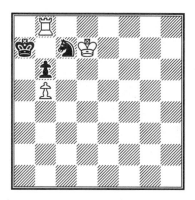

1.Ra8+!! Nxa8. 1...Kxa8; 2.Kxc7 Ka7; 3.Kc6 Ka8; 4.Kxb6 Kb8; 5.Kc6 reaches the same position. **2.Kc8 Nc7.** The only legal move. **3.Kxc7 Ka8; 4.Kxb6 Kb8; 5.Kc6. Black resigned.**

(17) ALEKHINE - EUWE
World Championship, 1937

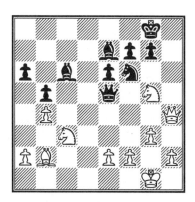

1.Qh8+ Kxh8; 2.Nxf7+ Kh7; 3.Nxe5 would have left White two pawns ahead and caused Black's imminent resignation.

(18) ALEKHINE - BOGOLJUBOW
Warsaw, 1941

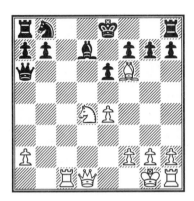

The kingside gets blasted open with **1.Nxe6 fxe6.** If 1...Bxe6;
2.Qd8# or 1...Qxe6; 2.Rc8+ Bxc8; 3.Qd8#. **2.Rc8+.** If now **2...Kf7.**
2...Bxc8; 3.Qd8+ Kf7; 4.Qe7+ Kg6; 5.Qxg7+ Kh5; 6.Qg5#.

3.Rxh8 gxf6. Or 3...Kxf6; 4.Qf3+ Ke5; 5.h4 mobilizing White's
king's rook when the lack of shelter for Black's king means that he
must soon lose. **4.Qh5+ Ke7; 5.Qc5+ Kf7; 6.Rxh7+ Kg8; 7.Qe7.**

(19) ALEKHINE - FREEMAN
USA, 1924

Our old friend, the back rank, is quickly exploited. **1.Re8+! Nf8;
2.Nh6+!! Qxh6; 3.Rxf8+ Kxf8; 4.Qd8#.**

ANSWERS TO THE PROBLEMS

(20) ALEKHINE - OPOCENSKY
Paris, 1925

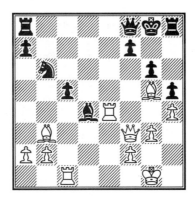

1.Rxd4 cxd4; 2.Rc6 Kh7. 2...Kg7; 3.Rxg6+! Kxg6. (3...fxg6; 4.Qb7+.) 4.Qf6+ Kh7; 5.Bxf7 Rg8; 6.Qf5+ Kg7; 7.Qg6+ Kh8; 8.Bf6+ Qg7; 9.Qh6#. **3.Bxf7 Rc8; 4.Rxg6. White wins.**

(21) EUWE - NAEGELI
Zurich, 1934

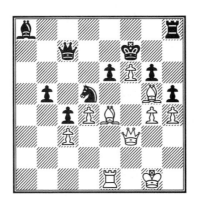

1.Bxg6+! Kxg6; 2.Qe4+ Kf7; 3.Qxe6+ Kg6. 3...Kf8; 4.Qe8#. **4.f7+ Kg7; 5.Bh6+! Rxh6; 6.f8Q+ Kxf8; 7.Qxh6+. Black resigned.** 7...Kf7; 8.Qh7+ Kf8; 9.Qh8+ Kf7; 10.Re5 and **White wins.**

(22) EUWE - NESTLER
Dubrovnik, 1950

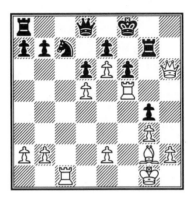

The f-file must be opened! **1.Rg5 fxg5; 2.Qh8+ Rg8; 3.Rf1+ Ke8; 4.Qxg8#.**

(23) EUWE - ROSSETTO
Buenos Aires, 1947

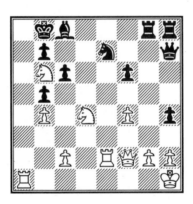

Before checking at a8, you need to take away Black's flight square at c7. **1.Nxb5! cxb5; 2.Qc5! Nc6; 3.Qd6+ Qc7; 4.Ra8#.**

ANSWERS TO THE PROBLEMS

(24) TARRASCH - EUWE
Amsterdam, 1923

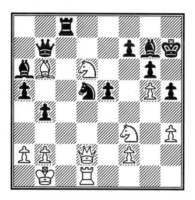

Black won with **1...Nc3+; 2.bxc3 Qxf3; 3.cxb4 Rc6; 4.Bxa5 Be2; 5.b5 Rxd6.**

(25) BOTVINNIK - KERES
World Championship, The Hague, 1948

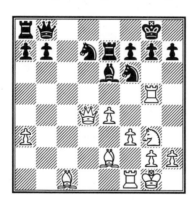

The fun begins with **1.Rxg7+!! Kxg7.** 1...Kh8; 2.Bh6 Qe5; 3.Qxe5 Nxe5; 4.f4 Neg4; 5.Bxg4 Nxg4; 6.Bg5 Kxg7. (6...Rd7; 7.Nh5 followed by h3 and Bf6.) 7.Bxe7 and White has a serious material advantage. **2.Nh5+ Kg6.** 2...Kh8; 3.Bb2 wins a piece. **3.Qe3. Black resigned.**

(26) STOLBERG - BOTVINNIK
Soviet Championship 1940

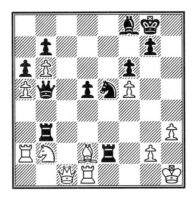

Black can win with the stunning **1...Rxh3+!; 2.gxh3 d4!** The queen uses the light-squared diagonal to enter the kingside and finish off the enemy king.

(27) GOGLIDZE - BOTVINNIK
Moscow, 1935

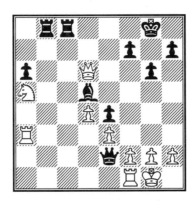

This time the two back ranks are needed. **1...Qxf1+; 2.Kxf1 Rb1+; 3.Ke2 Rc2#.**

(28) LILIENTHAL - BOTVINNIK
Moscow, 1941

It is not easy to spot **1...Rg2!!; 2.Qe4.** 1.Qxg2 Qh5#. **2...Rxh2+!; 3.Kxh2 Qh5+; 4.Kg2 Qxd1; 5.Bc4 h5** and Black won without much difficulty.

(29) SMYSLOV - HÜBNER
Candidates' Match, 1983

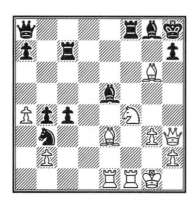

1.Bxh7 Rxh7; 2.Ng6+ Kg7; 3.Qd7+ Rf7; 4.Rxf7+ Bxf7; 5.Nxe5 Qd5; 6.Qxa7. White had an overwhelming advantage.

(30) SMYSLOV - DONNER
Havana, 1966

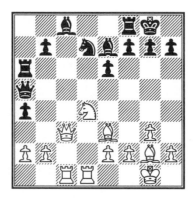

1.Qxa5 Rxa5; 2.Rxc8! Rxc8; 3.Bxb7 Re8; 4.Nc6 Rd5. 4...Rb5 would have been better, but even so White should win after 5.Nxe7+ Rxe7; 6.Bc6 Rxb2; 7.Bxd7 with the deadly threat of Bc5. **5.Nxe7+ Rxe7; 6.Bxd5 exd5; 7.Rxd5** and two extra pawns are too much.

(31) SMYSLOV - FLOHR
Soviet Championship, 1949

Mating combinations in the endgame? Why not! **1.g6+! hxg6; 2.Rb7#.** More resistance is provided by 1...Kxg6, but after 2.Rg1+ checkmate cannot be avoided. 2...Kh6; 3.Kf6 Kh5. (3...Rh3; 4.Rg6+ Kh5; 5.Rh8 wins.) 4.Rg5+ Kh4; 5.Rh8 Rxc6; 6.Rxh7# nor 2...Kf7; 3.Rcg8 Rxc6; 4.R1g7#.

(32) SMYSLOV - KOTTNAUER
Moscow, 1948

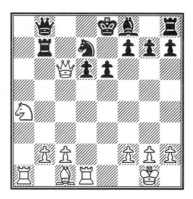

1.Nc5! dxc5; 1...Rc7; 2.Nxd7 Rxd7; 3.Ra8 and **White wins**.
2.Bf4! Even stronger than 2.Rxd7 Rxd7; 3 Ra8 which picks up
Black's queen for two rooks, and still leaves Black's king stranded
in the center. **2...Bd6.** 2...Qxf4; 3.Qc8+ Ke7; 4.Qxb7 with a win.
3.Bxd6 Rb6; 4.Qxd7+! and Black loses after **4...Kxd7; 5.Bxb8+.**

(33) TUKMAKOV - TAL
Soviet Championship, 1969

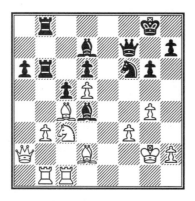

1...Nxg4!; 2.Ne4 2.fxg4 Qf2+; 3.Kh1 Qf3#. **2...Ne5** and **White
resigned**. The f3-square is weak, and ...Nxc4 threatens to exploit
the pin on the b-file, for example: 3.Rf1. (3.Be2 Qf5.) 3...Nxc4;
4.bxc4 Rb2; 5.Rxb2 Rxb2; 6.Qxa6 Qf5; 7.Qxd6 Qh3+; 8.Kh1 Qxf1#.

(34) TAL - MALICH
Varna, 1958

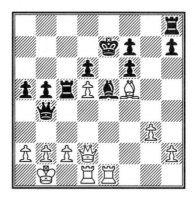

White wins with **1.Rxe5+!!.** Black tried **1...fxe5** since 1...dxe5 loses to 2.d6+, and after 2...Ke8; 3.d7+ Kd8; 4.Qd6 or 2...Kd8; 3.Qh6 there is no defense. **2.Qg5+ Kf8.** 2...Ke8; 3.Qf6 and 2...f6 3.Qg7+ also win without difficulty. **3.Qf6 Rg8; 4.Be6. Black resigned.**

If Black defends the f-pawn with either rook, then Qd8+ wins.

(35) TAL - PARMA
Bled, 1961

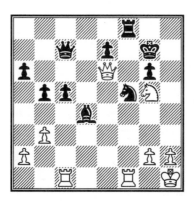

The fork at e6 can hardly be missed, so the queen merely has to evacuate that square with a threat or capture. **1.Qxf5! Rxf5; 2.Ne6+.**

ANSWERS TO THE PROBLEMS

(36) TAL - SOLOMIS
Soviet Union, 1970

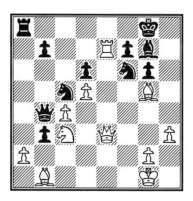

This is somewhat complicated. White must break down the door before Black cleans up on the queenside. **1.Bxg6! bxa2.** 1...fxg6; 2.Rxg7+! Kxg7; 3.Qe7+ Kg8; 4.Bxf6 and **White wins. 2.Bxf6 a1Q+.** 2...Bxf6; 3.Qh6 and **White wins. 3.Kh2 Qaxc3; 4.Bxf7+ Kh7; 5.Bg6+! Kh8.** 5...Kg8; 6.Rxg7+ Kh8 (6...Kf8; 7.Qe7#) 7.Qh6#. **6.Qh6+ Kg8; 7.Qxg7#.**

(37) PETROSIAN - SPASSKY
World Championship, 1966

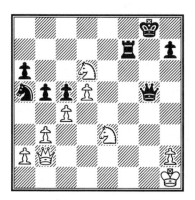

The fork again! **1.Qh8+ Kxh8; 2.Nxf7+.**

(38) PETROSIAN - IVKOV
USSR - Yugoslavia, 1979

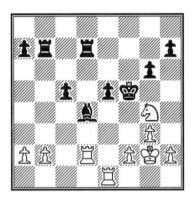

This hardly seems like the place for a mating combination, but the Black king is in mortal danger. **1.Rxd4! Rxd4; 2.Rxe5+ Kxg4; 3.f3#.**

(39) PETROSIAN - MOLDAGALIYEV
Soviet Union, 1969

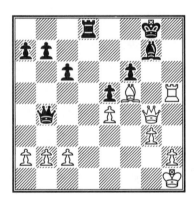

The f7-square is critical. **1.Rh8+!! Kxh8.** 1...Kf7; 2.Qg6+ Ke7; 3.Qxg7+ Kd6; 4.Rxd8+ and **White wins. 2.Qh5+ Kg8; 3.Be6+ Kf8; 4.Qf7#.**

(40) PETROSIAN - STEIN
Soviet Union, 1961

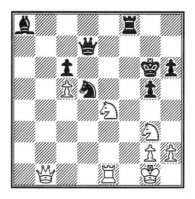

The knights provide the solution. **1.Nf6+! Kxf6.** 1...Kg7; 2.Qh7+ Kxf6; 3.Nh5#. **2.Nh5+ Kf7; 3.Qh7#.**

(41) SPASSKY - PFLEGER
Munich, 1979

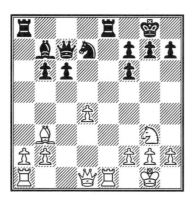

This combination leads to a hopeless position for Black. **1.Bxf7+ Kxf7; 2.Qh5+ g6.** If 2...Kf8; 3.Qxh7, and the threats of Nf5 and Nh5 oblige Black to transpose into the game. **3.Qxh7+ Kf8; 4.h4.** Amazingly, Black is completely hamstrung and has no defense to h5 when either White's h-pawn or his knight will enter the attack with decisive effect.

(42) SPASSKY - SMYSLOV
Bucharest, 1953

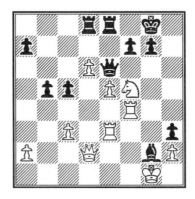

1.Nxg7 Rxd6. 1...Kxg7; 2.Rg3+ Kf8; 3.Rh4 gives White the point, as does 1...Qg6; 2.Nxe8 Bf3+; 3.Kf1 and Black has run out of useful moves. **2.Nxe6 Rxd2; 3.Rg3+ Kh7; 4.Rh4#.**

(43) SPASSKY - AVERKIN
Soviet Union, 1973

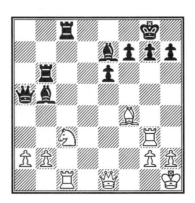

Getting to the g7-square takes some work on the other side of the board. **1.Bc7! Rxc7; 2.Qe5.**

(44) SPASSKY - DARGA
Varna Olympiad, 1962

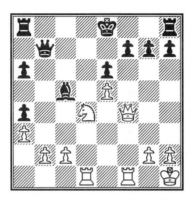

This is a nice long combination, which is sufficiently forced so that all complications can be worked out. **1.Nxe6! fxe6; 2.Qxa4+ Qb5.** 2...Ke7; 3.Qh4+ Ke8; 4.Qg4 Rf8. (4...Qe7; 5.Qa4+ Qd7; 6.Qxd7#.) 5.Qxe6+ Be7; 6.Rxf8+ Kxf8; 7.Rd7 and **White wins**. **3.Qg4 Qc6.** 3...Rf8; 4.Qxe6+ Be7; 5.Rxf8+ Kxf8; 6.c4! Qc5; 7.Rf1+ Ke8; 8.Qg8+ Bf8; 9.Qf7+ and **White wins**. **4.Qxg7 Rf8; 5.Rxf8+ Bxf8; 6.Qxh7 Rc8; 7.Qg6+.** Black resigned, because on 7.Qg6+ Ke7; 8.Rd6. White wins. 7...Ke7, the simple 8.Rd6 has threats at e6 and h7.

(45) FISCHER - DELY
Skopje, 1967

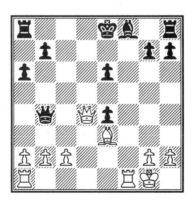

White gives up the exchange and control of the f-file, but the combined force of the queen and bishop on the diagonals, and the rook which moves from a1 to the open d-file, is overpowering.

1.Rxf8+! Qxf8; 2.Qa4+ b5. 2...Ke7 drops the queen to 3.Bc5+. 2...Kd8 takes longer to defeat, but the win is straightforward, and it is mate in eight! 3.Rd1+ Kc7; 4.Qc4+ Kb8; 5.Rd7 Qc8; 6.Bf4+ Ka7; 7.Qd4+ Qc5; 8.Qxc5#. **3.Qxe4 Rd8.** 3...Rc8; 4.Qxe6+ Kd8; 5.Rd1+ Kc7; 6.Qb6#. **4.Qc6+ Rd7; 5.Rd1 Qe7; 6.Bg5. Black resigned.**

(46) FISCHER - MIAGMASUREN
Sousse, 1967

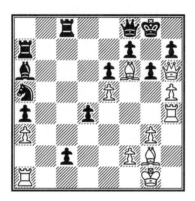

A classic case of parting with the lady. **1.Qxh7+!** Here **Black resigned** because 1...Kxh7; 2.hxg6+ Kxg6. (2...Kg8; 3.Rh8#.) 3.Be4#.

(47) BISGUIER - FISCHER
New York, 1960

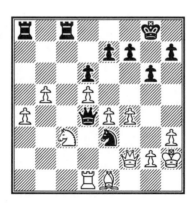

1...Qxc3!; 2.Bxc3 Nxd1; 3.Qd4 Nxc3. The two rooks and knight are more than a match for the exposed queenside pawns. **4.b6 Rc5;**

5.e5 Rxa4; 6.b7. The b-pawn will promote, but none of its colleagues will. **6...Rxd4; 7.b8Q+ Kg7; 8.exd6 exd6; 9.Qxd6 Rcxd5** and **White resigned** a few moves later.

(48) CARDOSO - FISCHER
New York, 1957

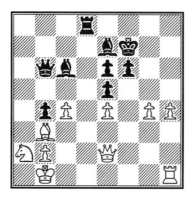

1...Rd2; 2.Qxd2 Bxe4+; 3.Bc2 Bxh1; 4.Qh6 Qg1+; 5.Nc1 Qxg4 and Black had an extra pawn and the bishop pair. The queen defends the critical squares on the g-file. After **6.Qh7+ Qg7; 7.Qh5+ Kf8; 8.Ba4.** Fischer brought the light squared bishop back into the game with **8...Be4+; 9.Ka1 Bg6** and went on to win.

(49) KARPOV - ALBURT
Malta Olympiad, 1980

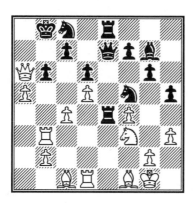

Alburt was not exactly confident going into his game against the World Champion, but he surely didn't expect to get blown away quickly with **1.c5! dxc5; 2.Bb5 c6; 3.Bxc6 Bd4+; 4.Nxd4 Nxd4; 5.axb6 Nf3+; 6.Rxf3 Re1+; 7.Rxe1. Black resigned.**

(50) KARPOV - OFIESH
Simultaneous Exhibition, 1991

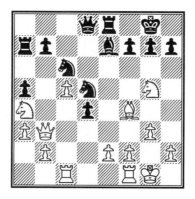

A long but effective combination. **1.Nxf7!** A beautiful move to see in a simulation. **1...Kxf7; 2.Nb6** deftly exploits the pin. **2...Ke6; 3.e4! dxe3; 4.Rfe1 Nd4; 5.Rxe3+ Kf7; 6.Qxd5+ Qxd5; 7.Nxd5 Ne6; 8.Rxe6 Kxe6; 9.Nc7+. Black resigned.**

(51) KARPOV - CSOM
Bad Lauterberg, 1977

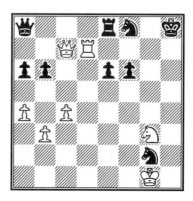

Looking at the seventh rank, we know the end is near. The queen needs to move to the head of the queue, but must use a circuitous

route. **1.Nf5! Nxd7.** 1...exf5; 2.Qh2+ Kg8; 3.Qg3+ Kh8; 4.Qg7#.
1...Qb8; 2.Rh7+ Nxh7; 3.Qg7#. **2.Qh2+ Kg8; 3.Qg3+ Kf7; 4.Qg7#.**

(52) TARJAN - KARPOV
Skopje, 1976

Black forces mate, or the win of all White's pieces. 2.fxe3 Qg3#.
White can bail out with 2.Qf3, but 2...Rxf3+; 3.gfx3 Qxf5+ is hardly
worth sticking around for. **2...Rxg3+; 3.Kh2 Qxf2+; 4.Kh1 Rg1#.**
4...Qg1#.

(53) KASPAROV - BROWNE
Banja Luka, 1979

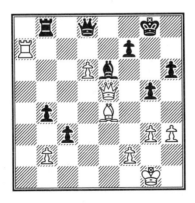

Kasparov wasn't even a Grandmaster yet, but this combination
should be spotted even by an amateur player. **1.Bh7+ Kxh7; 2.Qxe6.**

(54) KASPAROV - MARTINOVIC
Baku, 1980

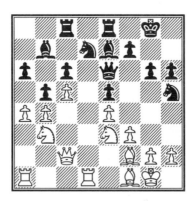

There are definite similarities between this position and Morphy's exploitation of de Riviere's queen situation in combination number 3. **1.Nc4!** A tactical blow in the interests of advancing White's strategic cause.

1...Rc7. 1...bxc4?; 2.Bxc4 Qf6; 3.Rxd7 Rb8; 4.Na5 Bc8; 5.Rc7 Rxb4; 6.Nxc6! Rb7; 7.Nxe7+ and White wins. **2.Nd6 Rb8; 3.axb5 cxb5; 4.Nxb7 Rbxb7; 5.Qa2!** and it is all over but the shouting. **Black resigned** after another ten moves.

(55) KASPAROV - KARPOV
World Championship, 1985

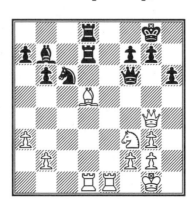

Karpov blundered into this position, one of his worst tactical oversights. He missed. **1.Qxd7 Rxd7; 2.Re8+ Kh7; 3.Be4+. Black**

resigned. After 3...g6; 4. Rxd7 Ba6; 5. Bxc6 Qxc6; 6. Rxf7 is **checkmate**. In all alternative lines Black loses massive amounts of material.

(56) KASPAROV - LARSO
Exhibition Internet, 1995

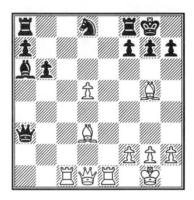

Yes, there are combinations in cyberspace! **1.Bxh7+! Kxh7; 2.Be7 Qd3; 3.Qh5+.** 3.Bxf8 is only slightly better for White, because Black has dangerous connected passed pawns on the queenside after, say 3...Nb7; 4.Bb4 Rd8 with counterplay. **3...Kg8; 4.Bxf8 Nb7.** 4...Kxf8; 5.Qh8#. **5.Be7 Bc4; 6.d6 Nd8; 7.Bxd8 Rxd8; 7.Qh4!** and **Black resigned** a few moves later.

18. RECOMMENDED READING

Alekhine, Alexander. *My Best Games.* Batsford.

Burger, Robert. *The Chess of Bobby Fischer.* Hypermodern Press.

Capablanca, Jose R. *Last Lectures.*

Divinksy, Nathan & Raymond Keene. *Warriors of the Mind.* Harding & Simpole.

Euwe, Max. *Strategy and Tactics in Chess.*

Euwe, Max. *From My Games.* Dover.

Fischer, Robert J. *My 60 Memorable Games.* Batsford.

Kasparov, Garry. *The Test of Time.* Cadogan.

Kasparov., Garry et. al. *Fighting Chess.* Batsford.

Mednis, Edmar. *How Karpov Wins.* McKay.

Petrosian, Tigran. *Petrosian's Legacy.* Editions Erebouni.

Réti, Richard. *Masters of the Chessboard.* Dover.

Schiller, Eric. *The Big Book of Combinations.* Hypermodern Press.

Schiller, Eric. *World Champion Openings.* Cardoza Publishing.

Smyslov, Vasily. *Endgame Virtuoso.* Cadogan.

Steinitz, Wilhelm. *Modern Chess Instructor.* Edition Olms.

Tal, Mikhail & Viktor Khenkin. *Tal's Winning Chess Combinations.* Simon & Schuster.

Tangborn, Eric. *Combinations of the World Champions.* Chess Digest.

19. INDEX OF GAMES AND EXERCISES

CARDOZA PUBLISHING CHESS BOOKS

- OPENINGS -

WINNING CHESS OPENINGS *by Bill Robertie* - Shows concepts and best opening moves of more than 25 essential openings from Black's and White's perspectives: King's Gambit, Center Game, Scotch Game, Giucco Piano, Vienna Game, Bishop's Opening, Ruy Lopez, French, Caro-Kann, Sicilian, Alekhine, Pirc, Modern, Queen's Gambit, Nimzo-Indian, Queen's Indian, Dutch, King's Indian, Benoni, English, Bird's, Reti's, and King's Indian Attack. Examples from 25 grandmasters and champions including Fischer and Kasparov. 144 pages, $9.95

WORLD CHAMPION OPENINGS *by Eric Schiller* - This serious reference work covers the essential opening theory and moves of every major chess opening and variation as played by *all* the world champions. Reading as much like an encyclopedia of the must-know openings crucial to every chess player's knowledge as a powerful tool showing the insights, concepts and secrets as used by the greatest players of all time, *World Champion Openings (WCO)* covers an astounding 100 crucial openings in full conceptual detail (with 100 actual games from the champions themselves)! *A must-have book for serious chess players.* 384 pages, $18.95

STANDARD CHESS OPENINGS *by Eric Schiller* - The new definitive standard on opening chess play in the 20th century, this comprehensive guide covers every important chess opening and variation ever played and currently in vogue. In all, more than 3,000 opening strategies are presented! Differing from previous opening books which rely almost exclusively on bare notation, *SCO* features substantial discussion and analysis on each opening so that you learn and understand the concepts behind them. Includes more than 250 completely annotated games (including a game representative of each major opening) and more than 1,000 diagrams! For modern players at any level, this is the standard reference book necessary for competitive play. 768 pages, $24.95

UNORTHODOX CHESS OPENINGS *by Eric Schiller* - The exciting guide to all the major unorthodox openings used by chess players, contains more than 1,500 weird, contentious, controversial, unconventional, arrogant, and outright strange opening strategies. From their tricky tactical surprises to their bizarre names, these openings fly in the face of tradition. You'll meet such openings as the Orangutang, Raptor Variation, Halloween Gambit, Double Duck, Frankenstein-Dracula Variation, and even the Drunken King! These openings are a sexy and exotic way to spice up a game and a great weapon to spring on unsuspecting and often unprepared opponents. More than 750 diagrams show essential positions. 528 pages, $24.95

GAMBIT OPENING REPERTOIRE FOR WHITE *by Eric Schiller* - Chessplayers who enjoy attacking from the very first move are rewarded here with a powerful repertoire of brilliant gambits. Starting off with 1.e4 or 1.d4 and then using such sharp weapons such as the Göring Gambit (Accepted and Declined), Halasz Gambit, Alapin Gambit, Ulysses Gambit, Short Attack and many more, to put great pressure on opponents, Schiller presents a complete attacking repertoire to use against the most popular defenses, including the Sicilian, French, Scandinavian, Caro-Kann, Pirc, Alekhine, and other Open Game positions. 192 pages, $14.95.

GAMBIT OPENING REPERTOIRE FOR BLACK *by Eric Schiller* - For players that like exciting no-holds-barred chess, this versatile gambit repertoire shows Black how to take charge with aggressive attacking defenses against any orthodox first White opening move; 1.e4, 1.d4 and 1.c4. Learn the Scandinavian Gambit against 1.e4, the Schara Gambit and Queen's Gambit Declined variations against 1.d4, and some flank and unorthodox gambits also. Black learns the secrets of seizing the initiative from White's hands, usually by investing a pawn or two, to begin powerful attacks that can send White to early defeat. 176 pages, $14.95.

COMPLETE DEFENSE TO QUEEN PAWN OPENINGS *by Eric Schiller* - This aggressive counterattacking repertoire covers Black opening systems against virtually every chess opening except for 1.e4 (including most flank games), based on the exciting and powerful Tarrasch Defense, an opening that helped bring Championship titles to Kasparov and Spassky. Black learns to effectively use the Classical Tarrasch, Symmetrical Tarrasch, Asymmetrical Tarrasch, Marshall and Tarrasch Gambits, and Tarrasch without Nc3, to achieve an early equality or even an outright advantage in the first few moves. 288 pages, $16.95.

COMPLETE DEFENSE TO KING PAWN OPENINGS *by Eric Schiller* - Learn a complete defensive system against 1.e4. This powerful repertoire not only limits White's ability to obtain any significant opening advantage but allows Black to adopt the flexible Caro-Kann formation, the favorite weapon of many of the greatest chess players. All White's options are explained in detail, and a plan is given for Black to combat them all. Analysis is up-to-date and backed by examples drawn from games of top stars. 288 pages, $16.95.

SECRETS OF THE SICILIAN DRAGON by *GM Eduard Gufeld and Eric Schiller* - The mighty Dragon Variation of the Sicilian Defense is one of the most exciting openings in chess. Everything from opening piece formation to the endgame, including clear explanations of all the key strategic and tactical ideas, is covered in full conceptual detail. Instead of memorizing a jungle of variations, you learn the really important ideas behind the opening, and how to adapt them at the chessboard. Special sections on the heroes of the Dragon show how the greatest players handle the opening. The most instructive book on the Dragon written! 208 pages, $14.95.

- MIDDLEGAME/TACTICS/WINNING CONCEPTS -

WORLD CHAMPION COMBINATIONS by *Keene and Schiller* - Learn the insights, concepts and moves of the greatest combinations ever by the greatest players who ever lived. From Morphy to Alekhine, to Fischer to Kasparov, the incredible combinations and brilliant sacrifices of the 13 World Champions are collected here in the most insightful combinations book written. Packed with fascinating strategems, 50 annotated games, and great practical advice for your own games, this is a great companion guide to *World Champion Openings*. 288 pages, $16.95.

WINNING CHESS TACTICS by *Bill Robertie* - 14 chapters of winning tactical concepts show the complete explanations and thinking behind every tactical concept: pins, single and double forks, double attacks, skewers, discovered and double checks, multiple threats - and other crushing tactics to gain an immediate edge over opponents. Learn the power tools of tactical play to become a stronger player. Includes guide to chess notation. 128 pages, $9.95

ENCYCLOPEDIA OF CHESS WISDOM, The Essential Concepts and Strategies of Smart Chess Play by *Eric Schiller* - The most important concepts, strategies, tactics, wisdom, and thinking that every chessplayer must know, plus the gold nuggets of knowledge behind every attack and defense, is collected together in one highly focused volume. From opening, middle and endgame strategy, to psychological warfare and tournament tactics, the *Encyclopedia of Chess Wisdom* forms the blueprint of power play and advantage at the chess board. Step-by-step, the reader is taken through the thinking behind each essential concept, and through examples, discussions, and diagrams, shown the full impact on the game's direction. You even learn how to correctly study chess to become a chess master. 400 pages, $19.95.

- BASIC CHESS BOOKS -

THE BASICS OF WINNING CHESS by *Jacob Cantrell* - A great first book of chess, in one easy reading, beginner's learn the moves of the pieces, the basic rules and principles of play, the standard openings, and both Algebraic and English chess notation. The basic ideas of the winning concepts and strategies of middle and end game play are shown as well. Includes example games of great champions. 64 pages, $4.95.

BEGINNING CHESS PLAY by *Bill Robertie* - Step-by-step approach uses 113 diagrams to teach novices the basic principles of chess. Covers opening, middle and end game strategies, principles of development, pawn structure, checkmates, openings and defenses, how to write and read chess notation, join a chess club, play in tournaments, use a chess clock, and get rated. Two annotated games illlustrate strategic thinking for easy learning. 144 pages, $9.95

- MATES & ENDGAMES -

303 TRICKY CHECKMATES by *Fred Wilson and Bruce Alberston* - Both a fascinating challenge and great training tool, this collection of two, three and bonus four move checkmates is great for advanced beginning, intermediate and expert players. Mates are in order of difficulty, from the simple to very complex positions. Learn the standard patterns and stratagems for cornering the king: corridor and support mates, attraction and deflection sacrifices, pins and annihilation, the quiet move, and the dreaded *zugzwang*. Examples, drawn from actual games, illustrate a wide range of chess tactics from old classics right up to the 1990's. 192 pages, $12.95.

MASTER CHECKMATE STRATEGY by *Bill Robertie* - Learn the basic combinations, plus advanced, surprising and unconventional mates, the most effective pieces needed to win, and how to mate opponents with just a pawn advantage. also, how to work two rooks into an unstoppable attack; how to wield a queen advantage with deadly intent; how to coordinate pieces of differing strengths into indefensible positions of their opponents; when it's best to have a knight, and when a bishop to win. 144 pages, $9.95

BASIC ENDGAME STRATEGY: Kings, Pawns and Minor Pieces by *Bill Robertie* - Learn the mating principles and combinations needed to finish off opponents. From the four basic checkmates using the King with the queen, rook, two bishops, and bishop/knight combinations, to the King/pawn, King/Knight and King/Bishop endgames, you'll learn the essentials of translating small edges into decisive checkmates. Learn the 50-move rule, and the combinations of pieces that can't force a mate against a lone King. 144 pages, $12.95.

BASIC ENDGAME STRATEGY: Rooks and Queens by Bill Robertie - The companion guide to *Basic Endgame Strategy: Kings, Pawns and Minor Pieces*, you'll learn the basic mating principles and combinations of the Queen and Rook with King, how to turn middlegame advantages into victories, by creating passed pawns, using the King as a weapon, clearing the way for rook mates, and other endgame combinations. 144 pages, $12.95.

EXCELLENT CHESS BOOKS - OTHER PUBLISHERS
- OPENINGS -

HOW TO PLAY THE TORRE by *Eric Schiller* - One of Schiller's best-selling books, the 19 chapters on this fabulous and aggressive White opening (1. d4 Nf6; 2. Nf3 e6; 3. Bg5) will make opponents shudder and get you excited about chess all over again. Insightful analysis, completely annotated games get you ready to win! 210 pages, $17.50.

A BLACK DEFENSIVE SYSTEM WITH 1...D6 by *Andrew Soltis* - This Black reply - so rarely played that it doesn't even have a name - throws many opponents off their rote attack and can lead to a decisive positional advantage. Use this surprisingly strong system to give you the edge against unprepared opponents. 166 pages, $16.50.

BLACK TO PLAY CLASSICAL DEFENSES AND WIN by *Eric Schiller* - *Shows you how to develop a complete opening repertoire as black.* Emerge from *any* opening with a playable position, fighting for the center from the very first move. Defend against the Ruy Lopez, Italian Game, King's Gambit, King's Indian, many more. 166 pages, $16.50.

ROMANTIC KING'S GAMBIT IN GAMES & ANALYSIS by *Santasiere & Smith* - The most comprehensive collection of theory and games (137) on this adventurous opening is filled with annotations and "color" on the greatest King's Gambits played and the players. Makes you *want* to play! Very readable; packed with great concepts. 233 pages, $17.50.

WHITE TO PLAY 1.E4 AND WIN by *Eric Schiller* - *Shows you how to develop a complete opening system as white beginning 1. e4.* Learn the recommended opening lines to all the major systems as white, and how to handle any defense black throws back. Covers the Sicilian, French, Caro-Kann, Scandinavia; many more. 166 pages, $16.50.

BIG BOOK OF BUSTS by *Schiller & Watson* - Learn how to defend against 70 dangerous and annoying openings which are popular in amateur chess and can lead to defeat if unprepared, but can be refuted when you know how to take opponents off their favorite lines. Greet opponents with your own surprises! Recommended. 293 pages, $22.95.

MIDDLEGAME/TACTICS/WINNING CONCEPTS -

CHESS TACTICS FOR ADVANCED PLAYERS by *Yuri Averbakh* - A great tactical book. Complex combinations are brilliantly simpified into basic, easy-to-understand concepts you can use to win. Learn the underlying structure of piece harmony and fortify skills through numerous exercises. Very instructive, a must read. 328 pages, $17.50.

BIG BOOK OF COMBINATIONS by *Eric Schiller* - Test your tactical ability in 1,000 brilliant combinations from actual games spanning the history of chess. Includes various degrees of difficulty from the easiest to the most difficult combinations. Unlike other combination books, no hints are provided, so you'll have to work! 266 pages, $17.95.

STRATEGY FOR ADVANCED PLAYERS by *Eric Schiller* - For intermediate to advanced players, 45 insightful and very informative lessons illustrate the strategic and positional factors you need to know in middle and endgame play. Recommended highly as a tool to learn strategic chess and become a better player. 135 pages, $14.50.

HOW TO BECOME A CANDIDATE MASTER by *Alex Dunne* -The book that makes you *think* is packed with tips and inspiration; from a wide variety of openings in 50 fully annotated games to in-depth middle and end game discussions, the goal is to take your game up to the Expert level. A perennial favorite. 252 pages, $18.95.

- ENDGAMES -

ESSENTIAL CHESS ENDINGS EXPLAINED VOL. 1 by *Jeremy Silman* - This essential and enjoyable reference tool to mates and stalemates belongs in every chess player's library. Commentary on every move plus quizzes and many diagrams insure complete understanding. All basic positions covered, plus many advanced ones. 221 pages, $16.50.

ESSENTIAL CHESS ENDINGS EXPLAINED VOL. 2 by *Ken Smith* - This book assumes you know the basics of the 1st volume and takes you all the way to Master levels. Work through moves of 275 positions and learn as you go. There are explanations of every White and Black move so you know what's happening from both sides. 298 pages, $17.50.